Praise for *The End of Education as We Know It*

This is a radical book. The current educational system is a part of the problem; we need a new education which could be a part of the solution. Ida Rose Florez is a visionary writer, explaining how the present educational system has become outdated and dangerous, and then outlining a new direction for education which is fit for the future. All parents and teachers should read it!

— Satish Kumar, founder and president emeritus,
Schumacher College and author, *Elegant Simplicity*

Ida Rose Florez challenges us to think about schools and education in ways that are unfamiliar to most. She introduces what to most of us is a new vocabulary for such thinking, to which we may feel some resistance. I urge you, experience and acknowledge the resistance, but don't let it stop you.

— Peter Gray, from the Foreword

The End of Education as We Know It is both fierce and practical—a toolkit for creating regenerative schools from the ground up. Whether you're a classroom teacher or an education policymaker, this book will equip you with methods and strategies to disrupt outdated assumptions, foster humanity in learning, and embrace the complexity of both children and the world they inhabit. This book is not about tepid tweaks and timid reforms. More boldly, Florez calls for an entirely new way of doing school, one that aligns with the demands of the world our kids will own.

— Jim Rietmulder, The Circle School
and author, *When Kids Rule the School*

This work beautifully and brilliantly achieves its noble ambition: We must learn to see differently to create the new forms of education so desperately needed. In great detail, and with gentle, insistent clarity, Ida Rose illuminates the damaging impact of the mechanistic worldview. And of equal importance, she calls us to take responsibility for changing both our worldviews and how we do our work. The combination of explanation, evocation, and invocation is very powerful.

— Margaret J. Wheatley, author of 12 books from
Leadership and the New Science (1992) to *Restoring Sanity* (2024)

The very act of reading Ida Rose's new book is an act of personal regeneration! Read this book slowly, take walks in the woods between chapters. Reflect on how Ida Rose effortlessly weaves personal stories and deeply meaningful analysis of our broken educational "machine" into the wisdom of our shared need for authentic, harmonious change. This is required reading for all who care about our future and about our responsibility to create a better world today.

— Illah Nourbakhsh, Ph.D., Kavčić-Moura Professor of Computer Science, Carnegie Mellon University Robotic Institute

Dr. Florez takes readers on a personal and poignant journey through our current, but antiquated, approach to education, while contrasting the one we all know so well with one that actually reflects the nature of living things and how they and we and our children learn. It's a totally engaging read, which is much needed at this point in time. This book is a must read for parents, teachers, school administrators, and anyone interested in learning and thinking in our complex world. It probably won't happen, but all politicians should read this book, as well.

— Jeffrey W. Bloom, Ph.D., Researcher & Advisory Board Member of the International Bateson Institute; Professor Emeritus, Northern Arizona University; author, *Creating a Classroom of Young Scientists*

A captivating must-read for anyone who is dissatisfied with the status quo of schools but not quite sure where to begin. Ida Rose Florez provides readers with the necessary foundation for transformation toward healing and humanity at its core.

— Francesca Lopez, Ph.D., Waterbury Chair in Equity Pedagogy and Professor of Education, Penn State University, College of Education

How better will the world be when regenerative education is the norm? Ida Rose Florez gives more than a glimmer of this as a possibility, she tells us a story of how it is being done, and the means by which it can grow to scale so every child of every location, in every language and cosmology becomes conversant with the embodied capacity of participatory earth-beings.

— Samuel Leguizamon Grant, Ph.D., Executive Director, Rainbow Research

The End of Education as We Know It grabs and keeps your attention with provocative, critical questions, and challenges you to consider and change your perspective and beliefs about education. Dr. Florez seamlessly weaves vivid and even humorous personal stories with clear, compelling descriptions of the neuroscience and systems concepts that undergird the re-visioning of education as regenerative learning. I highly recommend this guidebook/roadmap—for educators, parents, community members, students of science and systems, and anyone else who is ready to be challenged, to learn and grow, and to take action.

— Allison Titcomb, Ph.D., Chief Impact Officer & Senior Vice President, Community Development at United Way of Tucson and Southern Arizona

Okay! Are you ready to squirm? This book is a regenerative call to action. A rallying cry for educators to challenge the status quo, to be willing to squirm in the discomfort of change, and to engage in the messy, yet essential, work of reimagining education. Dr. Ida Rose strongly believes that we need to change the way we teach and learn by adopting a new approach that focuses on learning as a whole and engaging with community. The current education systems are outdated and based on old ways of thinking, and are not meeting the complex needs of our interconnected world. This new road map envisions a future where parents and teachers work together as co-educators, nurturing children's natural curiosity and independence, and where schools become dynamic community learning hubs that extend beyond traditional boundaries.

— Kahu (Rev.) Rennie Mau

The End of Education as We Know It is both inspiring and practical. The author's ability to explain complex processes in a way that is understandable to the reader is masterful. It should be required reading for every school administrator, politician, and teacher-education program in the country.

— Nanette (Sheri) Schonleber, Ph.D., Associate Professor Early Childhood Studies, Sonoma State University

Having always been bothered by educational assessment as seen from my context as a developmentalist, I am certain you will find, as I did, this book challenging and reaffirming. It reaffirms what you as an educator know to be true in your soul. The challenge will require you to consider your own beliefs about more than a century of "mechanistic" thinking. It will make you squirm. It will also give you hope.

— Linda Lee Arzoumanian, EdD, Pima County Arizona School Superintendent, Retired

Challenging times require challenging questions. Through her beautifully written narrative, Dr. Florez asks us to consider the challenging questions posed by our current educational system from a unique vantage point. A provocative read that tackles complexity through illustrative examples.

— Cori More, Ph.D., Department Chair, Associate Professor, Department of Special Education, Eastern Illinois University

Ida Rose Florez challenges those of us living under the spell of modernity to free ourselves and our children from the lethal limitations of complicated, reductionist, machine-based thinking—so prevalent in both schools and society. She offers insight and inspiration for a Great Turning towards an emergent, regenerative, systems-based way of thinking that honors the complexity and non-linearity of learning—and of life itself.

— Molly Brown, eco-philosopher; author, *Growing Whole: Self-Realization for the Great Turning*; co-author, *Coming Back to Life: The Updated Guide to the Work That Reconnects*

If a society is to have any chance of adapting to the radically different climate future we're facing, rethinking basic paradigms of how we learn and work together is an essential task. Ida Rose Florez's *The End of Education as We Know It* centers on childhood education systems. But the well-articulated insights and lessons it offers are relevant to anyone who seeks to reconstitute ways of being that build on the basic childhood values of wonder, curiosity, and deep reverence for the world and for one another.

— Peter Friederici, author, *Beyond Climate Breakdown: Envisioning New Stories of Radical Hope.*

The End of Education
As We Know It
Regenerative Learning for Complex Times

Ida Rose Florez, Ph.D.

Foreword by Peter Gray, Ph.D.

Cover design by Diane McIntosh.

Cover images: school corridor © iStock #1176489596,
group of students in forest © iStock 1210749865 monkeybusinessimages,
leaves in hallway © iStock #604836276 DNKSTUDIO

Printed in Canada. First printing, January 2025.

Any other inquiries can be directed by mail to:

New Society Publishers
P.O. Box 189, Gabriola Island, BC V0R 1X0, Canada
(250) 247-9737

LIBRARY AND ARCHIVES CANADA CATALOGUING IN PUBLICATION

Title: The end of education as we know it :
regenerative learning for complex times / Ida Rose Florez.

Names: Florez, Ida Rose, author.

Description: Includes index.

Identifiers: Canadiana (print) 20240456289 |
Canadiana (ebook) 20240456327 | ISBN 9781774060094 (softcover) |
ISBN 9781771423984 (EPUB) | ISBN 9781550928020 (PDF)

Subjects: LCSH: Educational change. | LCSH: Education—
Social aspects. | LCSH: Learning.

Classification: LCC LB2806 .F56 2025 | DDC 379—dc23

Funded by the Government of Canada | Financé par le gouvernement du Canada | Canada

New Society Publishers' mission is to publish books that contribute in fundamental
ways to building an ecologically sustainable and just society, and to do so with the
least possible impact on the environment, in a manner that models this vision.

Contents

In memory of
Sebreana Domingue, Connie Kral,
Greg Jung, and David Kukla.

Beloved educators.

Acknowledgments

I am grateful to have written this book while living and working on the ancestral lands of the Kumeyaay people, whose traditional lifeways intertwine with a worldview of earth and sky in a community of living beings. Currently I am blessed to live, work, and write on sacred land that has been inhabited by the Sinagua and Ancestral Pueblo for thousands of years. At present, the Zuni, Apache, Yavapai, Hualapai, Havasupai, Paiute, Diné, Hopi, and many other Arizona tribal nations recognize the land where I live as a significant spiritual place. I am thankful to call such beautiful and inspiring lands my home.

Writing a book, especially one on a topic that touches everyone, is never a solo journey. I am deeply grateful to New Society Publishers editor Caylie Graham for being this book's champion and for encouraging me every step of the way, and to everyone on the New Society team who have helped bring this book into the world. Traveling my authorship journey with me has been writing coach AJ Harper, and head cheerleader Laura Stone of Top Three Book Workshop along with too-many-to-name fellow authors and alums. Your camaraderie has made all the difference!

Much *mahalo* to Dr. Nicol Russel for consulting with me on the proper use of *'Ōlelo Hawai'i* (the Hawaiian language). I am forever grateful to Dr. Glenda Eoyang and Royce Holladay of the Human Systems Dynamics Institute for reviewing my application of Adaptive Action. Heartfelt thanks to Dan Duke, Tara Hurdle, and Dr. Sam Grant for their early feedback on the manuscript. Any omissions or errors are my own.

Thank you to my sons George and David, and their partners Niki and Kristian, for their loving support. I am grateful to my daughter Charissa for being a joy-to-work-with business partner, and her husband Jon for his love and hospitality. Finally, my deep gratitude to my husband Rick for reading everything I write more than once, for believing in me, and believing the world needs a whole new way of doing school.

Foreword

One measure of a good book, or at least of a certain kind of good book, is that it challenges our routine ways of thinking. It creates some discomfort. At least it does so if we really attend to it and think about it. Ida Rose Florez challenges us to think about schools and education in ways that are unfamiliar to most. She introduces what to most of us is a new vocabulary for such thinking, to which we may feel some resistance. I urge you, experience and acknowledge the resistance, but don't let it stop you.

Florez is passionately concerned with something that should concern us all: the way we are using up the resources of and despoiling the planet. Like many, she sees education as a key, maybe *the* key, to how the world can be saved. But unlike most other education reformers, she does not think this can be done by altering our current educational system.

Adding courses on ecology, modifying courses in social studies to highlight destructive policies, testing students on their understanding of the causes of climate change, requiring students to read about the ways of Indigenous People, adding courses on social-emotional learning or empathy—none of these, nor any other curriculum changes you or I might favor—will significantly alter our path of destruction. Other sorts of tinkering with the school structure—whether the physical layout of the building, the sizes of classes, the school calendar, or the tasks imposed on school personnel—won't do much either. The educational problem is much deeper than issues of curriculum or details of administration.

Our educational system is one that implicitly and unavoidably fosters a way of thinking about ourselves and our role in the world that is competitive, materialistic, hierarchical (correct answers come from those who have power over us), and ultimately disempowering (the system assumes we must be taught by drill because we can't figure things out ourselves). As Marshall McLuhan told us decades ago, "the medium is the message." Schools influence our thinking not only by the content of what they teach, but by the way they teach.

Florez believes, as do I, that real educational reform requires the death of the current system and replacement by new systems. She tells us that we don't have to kill the current system or even rail against it because it is already dying of natural causes. I would add that it is dying because it runs counter to the needs of the modern world and is causing increasingly obvious damage to the young people who go through it. Ever more people are recognizing the harm schools are doing to their children and are removing them for homeschooling or some other form of alternative schooling. Teachers, too, are quitting in ever greater numbers, and replacing them is becoming ever more difficult. It seems likely that the rate of such school attrition will accelerate over the next decade or two until schools as we know them become irrelevant.

As an evolutionary biologist, I am aware of two routes to change. One is the relatively gradual process of evolution, in which organisms change in form and behavior to meet new conditions. The other is extinction and replacement. The dinosaurs went extinct because they couldn't adapt to a dramatic global change that wiped out many species, including them. In contrast, some little mouse-like mammals survived the global change, evolved, and some of their lines eventually inhabited the ecological niches previously dominated by dinosaurs. Our current standard schools are the dinosaurs. Some of the little innovative schools we see scattered around the globe, founded on various new ideas, are the mice.

A key distinction at the core of Florez's book is that between *complicated* and *complex* systems. Complicated systems are those that contain many components, which act on one another in preplanned, predictable, cause-effect ways. Human-made machines, such as automobiles and computers, are complicated systems. They are planned by engineers and built by those who make the parts and put them together. If something goes wrong and you know enough about the system, you can identify the part that is not functioning correctly and fix or replace it.

All biological organisms, in contrast, are *complex* systems. Nobody built them. Rather, they evolved. As a key aspect of that evolution, they acquired ways of changing themselves to meet continuing challenges imposed by changes in the environment. They are self-organizing. They are, within limits, self-healing when something goes wrong. This is not to deny the value of Western medical science, which has found some valuable ways to help the self-healing processes of our complex body. But as every good physician knows, any alteration of the biological system can have unintended consequences, which emerge from the system's complexity. You give a drug to a person to reduce pain and maybe you cause addiction, or maybe you suppress a self-healing process in some unknown way.

Just as individual organisms (such as you and I) are complex systems, so are the formations or social structures resulting from connections among individuals interacting with one another. As Florez notes, a swarm of locusts is a complex system, as is a plaque of bacteria, as is a school or school district or department of education. This is why schools and the larger structures within which they are embedded are so resistant to attempts at reform. We can't alter them the way we might alter a machine, because the complexity precludes our ability to predict the consequence of any given intervention, and because the structures have evolved ways to repel foreign influences.

Our standard schools are complex systems, but they approach education as if it is complicated rather than complex. If education is complicated, then we should be able to build education into a person the way we might build an automobile. Indeed, the similarity between the way schools attempt to educate and the way automobiles are assembled is striking. In every school day, the students are sent, strictly by the clock, from one station (class) to the next, where a new component of "education" is added. A little math here, a little English grammar there, then some history, and so on. The assembly-line process is even more obvious in the year-to-year graded system of our schools. The child starts, with others of the same age group (the raw material), in kindergarten, and then is moved through 12 more year-long stops on the assembly line where, at each stop, new bits are added to each of the subject-matter components dictated by the curriculum. The goal is uniformity of product, each child in theory ends with the same education as all the others. That's not how real education works. That's not how our complex brains respond to experiences to create meaningful, adaptive, insightful mental progress.

Our schooling system completely ignores the fact that we humans evolved to learn by being curious and exploring, by developing interests, by pursuing those interests, and by playing—all of which are complex processes motivated from within. No teacher, no school system—nobody—can "educate" a person. Education always comes from within; it emerges from the person's interactions with the world around them. To facilitate education, we can set conditions that help students educate themselves, but we can't educate them, and we certainly can't expect that all students are going to learn the same things, at the same time, in the same way.

Florez provides us with a set of guidelines for planning a school or any organization that has a particular mission. The guidelines include thinking clearly about the mission of the organization, establishing the organization's boundaries (that is, who is in it and who is not), and setting up Simple Rules (which she capitalizes), which will keep the organization on track toward the desired mission while also providing ways for it to adapt to new conditions without losing the mission.

As I read and thought about Florez's guidelines, I found myself applying them to my understanding of the founding of a particular radically alternative school that I have spent some of my career observing and studying. The school was founded in 1968 and at this writing is still going strong. I'll conclude this foreword by describing the founding of that school through the lens of Florez's insights.

The founders of the school were a group who believed strongly in the principles of democracy. They believed that children growing up in a nation that prides itself in being democratic should acquire an understanding of democracy by experiencing it as they grow, not by reading about democracy or hearing lectures about it, forced upon them in an autocratic school. In an early statement of the school's intent, one of the founders pointed out that our standard schools are the least democratic institutions in the nation. He and the other founders believed that our nation's democracy would work better—would be more truly democratic—if children grew up experiencing, first hand, the privilege and responsibilities of democratic citizenship.

So, the first and primary Simple Rule of the planned school was that it would be run democratically by the school members. No member would have more official power than anyone else.

But who would be the school members? This is where boundary conditions had to be set. The founders knew of other innovative schools that fell apart because of disputes among parents, and they also believed that decisions should be made by those who are directly affected by those decisions, that is, by those regularly at the school. So, they decided that parents would not be school members. Parents could enroll their children or not, but they would have no vote on how the school operated. The school members would include only the staff and students. The students would be those, from age four through to the late teenage years, who enroll.

To ensure democracy going forward, the founders also set the rule that no staff members, including those founders who became staff members, would have tenure. They would all be on one-year contracts that would have to be renewed (or not renewed) each year by secret vote of all school members. They also chose to refrain from using the term "teacher" to refer to any of the staff, in the belief that in a democratic setting all are natural teachers and natural learners, regardless of age. They were also concerned that, because in typical schools teachers are classroom bosses, some might assume that anyone called a teacher at this school would be a boss. At this school there would be no bosses.

The founders also believed that the opportunity to play and explore in natural settings is a valuable educational asset. So, for the school's physical location, they purchased a large Victorian farmhouse with an adjacent barn, set on ten acres of land including a pond, next to a forested state park that could serve as addition to the school's campus.

That's pretty much it. Think of all the things they deliberately did NOT plan. They didn't purchase equipment in advance, beyond the sort of furnishings that might be found in any household. They did fill bookshelves with donated books and equipped the playroom with some donated toys. They didn't specify administrative positions or specific obligations of the staff. They didn't work out requirements for admissions, except that prospective students would have to be at least four years old and spend a visiting week at the school to be sure they liked it and to demonstrate they could care for themselves in that setting. They didn't work out any requirements for graduating, nor did they even discuss the question of whether or not the school would issue some kind of diploma. They didn't create any kind of curriculum, because they believed that students would learn in their own ways. If there would be any courses at all, they would be in response to student's requests.

So, the school was founded with certain startup conditions and boundaries, but it was not built. It emerged. All the many detailed policies, procedures, rules, and items of equipment required for the school to function well, as defined by its members, emerged from the democratic process. Because the democratic process is itself a process for change, the school has continued to evolve, for 56 years at the time of this writing, in response to changes in the interests and needs of its members and changes in society at large that have affected those needs and interests.

Studies of the graduates of this school, including one I conducted decades ago, indicate that they go on to successful lives. Many of them pursue careers that are direct extensions of passionate interests they developed in play at the school. Not surprisingly, they are generally less interested in making lots of money or achieving high status in some sort of power structure than are graduates of more typical schools. They are generally interested in pursuits that are both enjoyable and meaningful to them, where meaning often derives from the sense that they are adding to rather than subtracting from the long-term regeneration of society and the planet. Having taken responsibility for their own education and for administering the school as children, they go on to take responsibility for themselves and their surroundings as adults.

I have described the founding of a real school to provide a concrete example of some of the ideas in Florez's book, and to show that the ideas are not just pie-in-the-sky philosophy, but can be implemented to start a long-lasting school that works. This is far from the only example one might give, but it is the one I know best.

Now, go forth. Prepare yourself to think deeply. Turn the page and start reading Florez's lively and fascinating treatise on regenerative learning and the end of education as we know it.

— Peter Gray, Ph.D.

PART I

A Regenerative Future Starts with Schools

1

Buckle Up

Questioning of previously unnoticed assumptions can be painful, and many people resist it energetically. I sense I need the reader's goodwill in at least entertaining the idea of it.

~ Dr. Mary Midgley

Slowly, deeply, I breathed in Maui. It was early on an April day. Birdcalls filled the air as children stood with their *nā kumu a lākou* (teachers) facing east. A young girl blew a conch shell, inviting all to morning protocol. After a pause, a kumu raised her voice in an ancient *oli* (Hawaiian chant), welcoming the rising sun. Other kumu answered. The ageless words echoed between them, mingling with birdsong. The voices paused. Then the kumu lifted their voices as one and the children answered. As the last oli hung in the air, we stood quietly, the breeze whispering past our faces.

After a moment, the adults and children walked to a low-slung building, its green clapboard siding almost indistinguishable from the surrounding rainforest. I turned to follow, walking next to Kili, the school's director. The preschoolers climbed the steps, slipped off their shoes, and went inside.

At the bottom step a boy stopped and tapped the arm of a teacher wearing a yellow T-shirt, cuffed shorts, and flip-flops ("*slippahs*" on Maui). He spoke in *'Ōlelo Hawai'i* (the Hawaiian language). She responded in kind. Kili and I stopped.

"May I watch?" I whispered.

"Of course," Kili nodded, and headed up the stairs.

Pūnana Leo ʻO Maui is an ʻŌlelo Hawaiʻi immersion preschool nestled at the foot of the West Maui Mountains. A group of Hawaiian educators founded Pūnana Leo preschools in 1982 to revitalize the Hawaiian language and preserve their culture. At the time of my visit, I was Senior Director, Strategic Initiatives, with Arizona's statewide early childhood agency. Our organization worked with thirteen of the American Indian Tribes in Arizona. I was eager to learn the role ʻŌlelo Hawaiʻi immersion preschools played in preserving and revitalizing Hawaiian's indigenous language and culture. But I wasn't on the island for work. About a dozen years earlier I had lived on Maui, just a few miles from the school. I visit as often as I can. The island calls me back again and again.

E hoʻi mai ʻoe (come back).

I watched as the child at the bottom of the steps pointed to the ground and spoke in ʻŌlelo Hawaiʻi. The teacher, Kailani, responded by pointing, then saying a different word. The child, with puckered forehead, tilted his head and repeated it. Kailani responded and the child shook his head, rubbed his arm, and pointed at the ground. The back-and-forth continued like tennis. But this was no game. It was cultural resuscitation. Two learners breathing life back into an ancient language and culture.

Their language. Their culture.

Calling them back. E hoʻi mai ʻoe.

Regenerating what was almost lost forever.

After several exchanges, the child dropped to the ground, rolled over, and laid flat on his back. He raised his arm, pointed to it, then the ground, repeating a word Kailani had said. Kailani threw up her hands, exclaiming in delight. The boy jumped to his feet and hugged her. They joined hands and together walked up the steps.

I followed, slipping off my shoes just outside the door. They seemed enormous next to the row of little slippahs. Kili gestured for me to sit on a small chair toward the side of the class. Calendar time was starting. The children sat cross-legged and barefoot on a large woven mat, eyes focused on one of the older children, who stood speaking in ʻŌlelo Hawaiʻi. The lead child gestured toward two others who came forward as the child leader sat down.

The two children stood at opposite ends of a large wooden easel with a calendar of April taped on the front. The children led the lesson, using a pointer to tap the square representing each day as the class counted in ʻŌlelo Hawaiʻi. I have seen hundreds of calendar lessons. This was the first time I had seen children lead it.

I looked wide-eyed at Kili and mouthed, "That's impressive."

She leaned in and whispered, "The older children are rising kindergarteners. They're only with us a few more weeks. From the first day, children take responsibility for their own learning and for supporting others as we all learn together."

When they completed the lesson, I expected the class to move on to something else. Instead, the child leaders carefully spun the wooden easel around on its wheels. The reverse side held a poster of the lunar cycle surrounded by pictures of Maui's seashore and land, and the plants and animals that live in each.

Kili leaned over and whispered, "The *keiki* (children) learn both the Roman calendar and the Hawaiian lunar calendar." The children leading the lesson pointed to pictures of the lunar cycle as the class responded in ʻŌlelo Hawaiʻi. Kili continued, "The Hawaiian calendar teaches the patterns of the earth and sea and their relationship to the phases of the moon. The keiki learn what should be planted and harvested in each season and each lunar phase, and what is *kapu* (forbidden). The children learn that we live in cycles and relationships. They learn how respecting the cycles of the land and sea protect and nurture life. They learn to respect what is not to be taken so that life can flourish."

As the child leaders pointed to pictures of fish and plants, other children raised their hands and spoke in ʻŌlelo Hawaiʻi, their teachers and classmates nodding in recognition. In over two decades as a professional educator, I had never seen anything like it. Four- and five-year-old children easily discussing the cycles of life in their local ecosystem in a language that had nearly died a couple decades before.

I had only planned to stay an hour, but when the children began setting up lunch, I realized the morning was gone. Gently, almost imperceptibly, the happy chatter that had filled the morning faded to silence. A few children brought food to the tables and set places for each person to eat, all in silence. When they finished, the rest of the class sat down, paused for a moment, then began eating, also in silence.

While the children ate, Kili and I stepped outside. She explained that in keeping with Hawaiian tradition, they eat in silence. Silence allows space to pause and reflect on and be grateful for food, to contemplate where the food came from, and how human actions contribute to or disrupt the lifecycles that produce it.

I asked Kili how Pūnana Leo had been able to create a learning environment that did so much of what we know children need for healthy development, while empowering them to fully embrace their culture.

Kili smiled. "A school that centers on healthy Hawaiian ways will easily align with developmental science," she said. "Our ancestors raised people who navigated the open ocean in handbuilt wooden canoes. They had no radar, no sonar. They had their senses and their deep understanding of the ways in which Earth works. Our ancestors raised people who could discover new lands because they had keen observational skills. They could read the patterns of ocean currents, changes in the wind and rain, and, of course, the night sky. Once here, they knew how to observe the patterns of the land and the seashore. They knew how to learn to live in harmony with their new home and how to pass that knowledge on to future generations. Their keen observational skills weren't just for observing the land and the sea. They observed how humans grow and develop. Our ancestors would never have made it to Hawai'i or survived here very long if they didn't know how to raise children."

What If All Schools Were Like Pūnana Leo?

Kili and I sat in silence. I pondered what I'd seen that morning. Why couldn't all people have culturally rich and respectful learning experiences like those at Pūnana Leo? What if all schools valued and supported teaching in the ways we know children learn? Imagine if it was just assumed that children's cultural knowledge is critically important to their understanding of the way the world works?

Kili broke my reverie. "Our parents are future ancestors," she said. "We see them as fellow educators. All our parents prioritize learning ʻŌlelo Hawaiʻi as a family. Parents take language classes each week, donate workdays, and contribute their talents wherever they can."

What if teachers everywhere saw families as future elders and ancestors, laying the foundation of the legacy they will leave in their children? What if parents were embraced as fellow educators, with parenting and teaching valued as collaborative roles in preparing future generations to live bravely and responsibly in an increasingly complex world? Imagine parents fully engaged in their children's education alongside teachers who welcome their partnership as vital and necessary.

What if all schools believed even very young children could understand the lunar cycles and the relationship of Earth's cycles to sustainable agriculture? How different would our relationship with food be if every school taught deep mindfulness about what we eat and, from the earliest ages, taught that each of us has the responsibility to generate food in ways that nurture the land, not just to fill our bellies?

What would our society be like if right from the beginning, even before kindergarten, young children understood and accepted their own agency as learners? Imagine children expecting to have their voices respected and adults expecting to learn from children. How would our world be different if people of all ages, races, genders, languages, and sexual identities expected to be seen and heard and valued, and to see and hear each other?

Creating Regenerative Schools: the What, Why, and How

Since you're reading this book, you probably hold similar longings. You might be a parent who yearns to see your child love learning, or an educator who wants nothing more than the freedom to create experiences that support each child's unique interests. I have lived a long time in both those roles. Maybe, like me, you hunger to revitalize humanity's deep connection with Earth, or ache for people to care so deeply for our planet and all beings who live here that they adopt sustainable ways of living. These longings arise from our deep human need to belong, to be safe, and to care for one another. I wonder how much of our daily stress comes from collectively living in ways that fail to nurture these basic human needs.

Longings, especially deep longings, point us to *what* could be. They're a mark on the horizon by which we can set our compass. When it comes to actually creating the types of schools (and society) we want, the *what*, the longing, is not enough. We also need the *why* and the *how*.

Why is it that even with so many people yearning for dramatically different educational systems, things stay the same? Why is it that most schools simply don't teach the way we know people learn? Why is achievement measured in ways that don't measure learning? How do schools perpetuate racism, even when teachers and administrators abhor it? Why do girls and children of color receive inferior math and science instruction and far fewer opportunities to lead than white male students, even when white male teachers, parents, and policymakers agree it's wrong? How do we deal with entrenched and seemingly unmovable education systems?

We come back. We restore that which has been almost lost. E ho'i mai 'oe.

If we want longings to shape reality, the *why* and the *how* matter very much. Human motivations and behaviors are rooted in purpose and process—the *why* and the *how*. *Why* and *how* are the difference between great ideas gaining traction or floating away on the wind. I wrote this book because we urgently need a vastly different way to do school. And to get to that *what* we must organize ourselves around a collective understanding of the *why* and *how*. *Why* and *how* demand more from us than *what*. Imagining a different future together is necessary but relatively easy. The real effort comes when we organize around purposes and processes so intently that they take on a life of their own and transcend the limits of our imaginations.

Society and Schools Perpetuate Each Other

Keen awareness of Earth, its cycles, and relationships shows up in Pūnana Leo O Maui's children because for millennia, *Kanaka ʻŌiwi* (Indigenous Hawaiians) lived in close harmony with the sea and land. Pūnana Leo schools are not just language schools. The schools intentionally immerse children in both ʻŌlelo Hawaiʻi and *ka ʻike honua o Hawaiʻi*—a Hawaiian way of being in the world. How could it be otherwise? The way a society raises its young emerges from that society, from the values and assumptions that shape and structure the way people live together and define their culture. In Pūnana Leo schools, purpose sets conditions for process, and process emerges from purpose. The *why* and the *how* are inextricably connected.

The purpose and process that shape society don't flow in one direction. In an iterative cycle, education emerges from society, and society emerges from education. Raising young humans is the way societies replicate themselves. Whether carried out in institutions or in the everyday experiences of children in their homes and communities, education is how a society's ways of knowing, doing, and being are passed from generation to generation. If we want to understand a society, we must look at the educational systems that it shapes. If we want to understand an educational system, we must look at the society from which it emerges. They emulate each other.

The Mother System

For this reason, education is not merely one among many social institutions. Education is the Mother System. It is unique because of its nearly universal profound influence on the first years of life. Ensuring children learn the patterns of society early means those patterns become the deeply rooted, unquestioned "just the way things are." People learn what society expects about how to treat one another *at school*. People learn what society values *at school*. People learn what society says is vulgar or racist or mean (or not) *at school*.

Certainly, children learn values and expectations at home and in religious and other institutions. But the inherent purpose of education for the masses is for most of the population to internalize the assumptions and values of the society. We may all hold individual or family values, but at school, especially public school where nearly all North American residents are educated, students learn what is valued by society.

To care about schools is to care about society. Nearly every educator I know embraces their profession as noble. Teachers routinely push back against rules that constrain their freedom to teach well. If you are an educator, I ask you to push even further and join a vital group of people who sense the urgency of our time—people who value the Mother System as something more than a workforce pipeline. This book is about recognizing the vital role education plays in nurturing human capacity not only for individual success or corporate profit but for the benefit of all. A regenerative approach to learning takes the value of education to its rightful place: teaching the ways we, as a species, contribute to the continuation of life on Earth.

Education as We Know It Is Dangerously Frail

Education is not valued appropriately. The demoralizing status quo has taken its toll not only on children but on educators. The number of people choosing a career in education had plummeted even before the COVID-19 pandemic. According to the Learning Policy Institute, in 2019, for the first time ever, the demand for K–12 teachers in the United States outpaced supply by more than one hundred thousand. In December 2019, the Center for American Progress reported there were approximately 340,000 fewer people enrolled in teacher preparation programs in the 2016–2017 academic year compared to eight years earlier. In many locales, the outlook is even worse. According to the US Department of Education, thirty states experienced a decline of over 35 percent in enrollments in teacher preparation programs between 2010 and 2018.

Oklahoma saw an 80 percent drop.

The reasons for the decline are many. Low compensation has been identified as the primary culprit. Education careers across the entire field from childcare through higher education faculty positions pay about as much as jobs in the fast-food industry. A 2020 California Federation of Teachers analysis found masters and doctoral level adjunct faculty made annualized wages just over $32,000, with no benefits. In 2021, Berkeley's Center for the Study of Child Care Employment reported childcare workers' average hourly wage as $13.43, while preschool teachers with college degrees make just under $17.00/hour.

But is compensation the root problem? By many indicators, education as we know it—and therefore those who teach—are wildly successful. Over 90 percent of US children ages five to eighteen attend a public school. That means more than 90 percent of US-born adults did too. US educators can claim some remarkable accomplishments. They educated people who landed humans on the moon when television was still black-and-white and eradicated polio without a sequenced human genome. People educated in Western schools created COVID-19 vaccines in record time and kept schools going under the most trying of circumstances. Despite these successes, not only are teachers inadequately compensated but they also rarely get even a fraction of the credit they deserve for their contributions to society. Take the saying, "Those who can, do. Those who can't, teach." Woah. Why such contempt?

Undervaluing teachers is a symptom of something deeper. It's a part of the story nearly all of us have been trained to overlook—the *complexity* part of the story. Viewed through a complexity lens, what was once a robust envy-of-the-world institution is dangerously frail, but not because it has failed. Western education has exceeded all expectations at doing what it was intended to do: create a working class of people, educated just enough to make industrialized capitalism work.

Teachers are caught in the throes of this frail system that is teetering on the edge of collapse. For now, education as we know it continues, riding the coattails of its historic accomplishments, solidifying more and more around past success, growing increasingly rigid and perilously unable to adapt to the complex demands of our globally connected world. To most policymakers and pundits, fixing schools means shoring up funding, raising test scores, or reinventing teacher preparation. But to meet the complex challenges of our time, we don't need a fix. *We need an entirely different way of thinking about schools.*

Our way of thinking is *why* our schools remain unchanged. Changing our thinking is *how* we change them.

What if we thought about schools in an entirely new way? What if the word "school" didn't only mean a building down the street where kids go to learn? What if we redefine "school" to mean *any* place or time intentionally set aside for learning of *any* kind and for *any* age and collection of people?

With this definition, the Willow Bend Environmental Education Center in Flagstaff, Arizona, is a school. The Kōkua Learning Farm on Oahu, founded by Kim and Jack Johnson, is a school. An FFA or 4-H program is a school. The Exploratorium in San Francisco and a senior center offering Zumba are schools. A scout troop meeting in a leader's garage is a school. Our *lanai* on Maui where I homeschooled our kids and welcomed their neighborhood friends to learn with us on early release Wednesdays was a school. The Elementary Institute of Science in San Diego is a school. The homestead and sustainable living demonstration site my husband and I are creating near the Grand Canyon will be a school. What if we crack open the definition of school and shift our thinking a teensy bit? What possibilities, what freedoms, might that new thinking reveal?

New Thinking Makes Us Squirm

I shifted my weight and lifted my gaze from my iPad to the fluffy blanket of pink clouds out my window. I was only forty-five minutes into the four-hour flight home from Pittsburgh to San Diego and it already felt like hours. I stretched my neck and squirmed. Two thoughts kept rolling around, front of mind, like a used-car-dealership jingle I couldn't shake.

Creators of technology, not just consumers.

Wage peace, not war.

I was serving my second year as board vice president of the National Association for the Education of Young Children. Flying home from our retreat in Pittsburgh, I wanted to jot down some notes so I would remember details about the community-based early learning programs we had visited.

But I was distracted.

I kept thinking about what it meant to wage peace, not war, and what it meant for children to be creators of technology, not merely consumers.

I blame Dr. Illah Nourbakhsh for the distraction. A world-renowned Carnegie Mellon University professor of robotics, Illah spoke at our retreat's opening dinner. He told us about an app his students had created. When I think of computer science majors studying under one of the world's top roboticists, I don't picture them perched on child-sized chairs observing all the minute goings-on among three-year-old kids, but that's exactly what Illah's students did. They weren't looking to create teaching tricks or ideas for how a software program could train children to count or name colors. They were looking for ways preschoolers could use technology to support their own learning.

The app they created, *Message from Me*, fits the bill. When children want to share something they've seen or created at school, they use an iPad mini to take a video or pictures to text to loved ones. A child might text their mom pictures of their block creations, or show Nonna a worm in the school garden, or maybe introduce their brother to the class guinea pig. Teachers encourage children to narrate their pictures and video. Children love the app. Generating content that links home and school helps children focus on their experiences and practice language skills while creating opportunities for parents and teachers to support children's learning.

There was so much to love about *Message from Me*.

Still, I squirmed.

Children as creators, not merely consumers.

What a profound idea. I loved it. Well, I sort of loved it.

What did it mean for *my* work? At the time, I was the executive director of the Elementary Institute of Science in southeastern San Diego. I was passionate about the children in our predominantly working-class immigrant community getting their hands on the same technology as their affluent peers. We ran coding workshops, and I was working on starting a project to teach preschoolers beginning robotics. Still, I had to admit, when technology is in the hands of children, they are almost always responders, not creators. Most educational apps capture children's attention with intense animation, then drill for memorization of isolated facts. Kids might create an avatar from a short menu of options, but rarely does technology truly empower children to be agents of their own learning.

I was also a bit (admittedly self-righteously) annoyed. I was, after all, doing a heck of a lot more than what I saw others doing when it came to young children's equitable access to technology. Was it really my responsibility to ensure they were creators too?

I couldn't escape the notion that it was.

This dilemma alone would have kept me squirming all the way home, but I was even more nettled by the way Illah had started his presentation. It landed hard in my belly when he said it, and it still bugged me on the plane ride home.

"I use technology to wage peace, not war."

What in the world did that mean?

I had sometimes questioned the ethics of certain uses of military technology but hadn't given it deep consideration. I lived in San Diego. I was born there. San Diego is known for sunny beaches, surfers, and sailboats. But essentially, San Diego is a military town. My father, who was deployed from San Diego to the Pacific in WWII, wasted no time moving there from his hometown of Chicago after the war. He worked for and was laid off by nearly every defense contractor in the city. He's buried at Fort Rosecrans National Cemetery on the Point Loma peninsula, overlooking North Island Naval Air Station on Coronado. I grew up six miles south of Miramar—the military air base made famous by Tom Cruise in the movie *Top Gun*. I know all the best spots to watch the annual Blue Angels airshow.

I grew up assuming that keeping the peace is the morally justifiable purpose of superior military might—to so intimidate "bad actors" that they would never even consider picking a fight. But after 9/11 and with the wars in Iraq and Afghanistan dragging infinitely on, costing so many lives, traumatizing service personnel in ways that would never heal, ripping apart families, and devouring obscene amounts of money, I had begun to wonder if we had lost our way—or if insisting on military superiority was even ethical to begin with.

I couldn't shake Illah's remark. What does it even mean to *wage* peace? And what does technology have to do with it? These were new, uncomfortable questions for me.

I shifted my weight again, trying not to elbow the person in the middle seat, and looked back at my iPad. I decided to contemplate the whole waging peace thing later and opened an essay on paradigms written by the late biologist and systems thinker,

Dr. Donnella Meadows. I thought reading would distract me from my discomfort, but instead I squirmed even more. I read:

> The shared ideas in the minds of society, the great big unstated assumptions—unstated because they are unnecessary to state; everyone already knows them—constitute that society's paradigm, or deepest set of beliefs about how the world works. There is a difference between nouns and verbs. Money measures something real and has real meaning (therefore people who are paid less are literally worth less). Growth is good. Nature is a stock of resources to be converted to human purposes.... One can "own" land. Those are just a few of the paradigmatic assumptions of our current culture, all of which have utterly dumfounded other cultures, who thought them not the least bit obvious.

I stopped cold. No, *of course* nature isn't a stock of resources to be converted for human purposes; but *of course* you can own land. I *did* own land.

I had the paper to prove it.

I read the blog again. *Of course* money measures something and has real meaning. For one thing, it measures whether or not I can own land, right?

I wanted to argue more, but the Illah-sized lump in my gut tightened. I took a deep, focused breath. Maybe my own unquestioned assumptions were keeping me from seeing how peace and creativity were related. Maybe things I accepted as obvious truths, like the right to own land, were merely fabrications of the culture in which I was raised.

I felt caught in my own contradiction: Wasn't the belief that I could own land inextricably connected to seeing nature as a resource that I had a right to convert for my own purposes? Was there some connection between the right to own land and the necessity of military superiority? Might there be a connection between children consuming technology rather than being empowered by it and schools being so rigid they cannot adapt?

I sensed there was a bigger *why* that wove these threads together and that the *why* had a lot to do with *how* to move education to a better place. I also sensed the *why* and the *how* mattered very much. I spent the next nine years studying *why* and contemplating *how*. I share what I learned in this book.

No Easy Answers

This book is for people brave enough to squirm.

Since you're still reading, you're likely willing to remain buckled into discomfort long enough to candidly examine even the most taken-for-granted assumptions, not only about the way education works but the way the world works. This book is for people who, like me, are deeply disturbed that our schools remain entrenched in ways of teaching and learning that are obsolete and even inhumane. Grappling with the implications of these complex ideas demands courage. Whenever I consider the perils facing humanity and the planet on which we live, I want to look away.

No. That's not true. I want to *run* away.

Yet I know our times call for a critical mass of people to bravely contend with the connection between those dangers and education as we know it. Our society is at an inflection point. The machine paradigm has run its course. *Something will replace it*. This book is not only for people who want to change schools but also for people who want to shape the societal paradigm that emerges from the inflection point we're all living through, and who recognize that schools are a critical nexus for that change.

Biologist Dr. Donella Meadows, quoted above, had a lot to say about *how* to influence paradigms: "...you keep pointing at the anomalies and failures in the old paradigm, you keep coming yourself, and loudly and with assurance from the new one, you insert people with the new paradigm in places of public visibility and power. You don't waste time with reactionaries; rather you work with active change agents and with the vast middle ground of people who are open-minded."

This book is for active change agents and the vast middle ground of people who are open-minded about new ways of doing school. It is for people who want to create public and private options for learning that teach how to live in harmony with each other, with Earth, and all Earth holds. It is for people who want education systems to foster all learners' understanding of complex relationships, to prioritize mutual thriving, and to help learners create the conditions conducive to life. To get there, we need a movement of powerful changemakers who see clearly and act wisely under conditions of high complexity.

I've written this book to help you make sense of what you're experiencing, but I don't pretend to have easy or complete answers. Often there are no answers, only more questions. Hopefully better questions. There are rarely "solutions"—at least not in the way we typically define them. The ideas in this book are for people willing to be confused at times, perhaps even angry, and yet who stay buckled in and squirming. I've squirmed a lot as I've studied and written, not only because these ideas challenge my deeply held assumptions but because I know my insights run counter to many political and ideological positions, including my own. I can pretty much guarantee you'll find ideas you love and others you, well, don't.

Please know I'm in the same boat. I don't like some of the ideas I'm writing. I spent more than two decades building my career as an educational assessment expert. I've personally tested thousands of students. My doctorate in educational psychology is from one of the top-ranked programs in the country. My doctoral minor is in educational assessment. I've consulted with the National Governor's Association, helping states craft assessment policy. I've testified as a subject-matter expert in federal court about a mandated Arizona assessment that was revised based on my testimony. I've written articles on assessment published in peer-reviewed academic journals and for the UCLA Civil Rights project. I was clinical faculty at Penn State College of Medicine where I assessed children on the inpatient psychiatric unit and outpatient rehab and neurodevelopmental clinics. I developed and taught educational assessment courses at the University of Arizona and Arizona State.

After all of that, what I know beyond a doubt is that nearly all educational assessment is so grotesquely invalid, it should be forever banned. I've come to believe the subject of my decades of expertise should be (mostly) tossed into the garbage bin.

Ouch.

Writing this book also makes me squirm because I know that how I think about much of what I've written will change over time. When it comes to complexity, there is so much to learn. My thinking will evolve, others will have new and challenging ideas, and new discoveries will be made. Even though I don't have this all figured out, and I can't point to anyone who does, this is no time to be silent. We need new questions. We need conversations that invite courageous consideration of the relationship between our educational systems and the harm routinely done to people and planet.

I also squirm because many people want to know how to "change the world." I question if we *can* change the world, and besides, I'm asking you to do something harder. I am asking you to reconsider how you *understand* the world. I am asking you to be open to considering that ways of thinking and being that you've taken for granted or taken as sacred might in fact be disturbingly incomplete and even harmful. I am asking you to trust that from such openness new understandings will emerge that will lead to profound and powerful changes in you, your life, and your work. I am asking you to trust that when enough people do that, our society will adapt and become compatible with how the world actually works.

As a fellow traveler, I can assure you this isn't a casual stroll. I echo science philosopher Dr. Mary Midgley who said, "This questioning of previously unnoticed assumptions can be painful, and many people resist it energetically. I sense I need the reader's goodwill in at least entertaining the idea of it." Still, I can further assure you, if you read with an open mind and heart, by the end of this book you will have powerful new insights that will help you discern wise actions that you had never even thought about before. You'll see schools, their potential to shift society, and your role in the process in a whole new way.

Changing Society? Where to Begin?

In 1893, the United States was rapidly expanding its position as the primary engine driving the second wave of the industrial revolution. With the US hungry for sugar and cheap labor, and Hawai'i an ideal gateway for Asian immigration, the time had come for those who colonized the islands to overthrow its monarchy. Sanford B. Dole led the coup, unseating Queen Lili'uokalani and establishing a provincial government. US President Cleveland opposed annexing Hawai'i as a territory, but his successor, McKinley, saw Pearl Harbor as invaluable in the Spanish-American War, so he claimed the islands for the US. Shortly after congress approved annexation, Dole and his team set about Americanizing the islands in earnest. Overthrowing the monarchy was merely the first step. Colonizing the culture was the goal.

Where did they start? They started with schools.

At the time of the illegal annexation, over half a million people spoke 'Ōlelo Hawai'i and 90 percent of Hawaiians were literate. Three years after the coup, the provincial government outlawed teaching 'Ōlelo Hawai'i in schools. Eighty years later, only two thousand native speakers remained, a 99.6 percent decrease. Of those, only thirty-two were children.

In the 1970s, fearing the complete loss of his ancestral language, Larry Kimura, a young professor of linguistics and anthropology, rallied his students and other educators. They gathered on Friday nights, bumbling around the eloquent language their grandparents had spoken so melodically. Committing to speak only 'Ōlelo Hawai'i in their homes, within a few years their group included a handful of young children who were the first native speakers in decades. With a group of committed parents and educators prepared to reclaim their culture and their language, it was time to scale up cultural revitalization.

Where did they start? They started with schools.

Teaching ʻŌlelo Hawaiʻi remained illegal. Hawaiian high school students could study German or French, but not their ancestral language. Larry and his students did what Donella Meadows recommended. They kept speaking loudly and with the full assurance of their position. In 1978, the Hawaiian government amended its constitution, making Hawaiʻi the only US state with two official languages. Four years later, Pūnana Leo schools opened, committing to a simple vision: *E Ola Ka* ʻŌlelo Hawaiʻi (the Hawaiian language shall live). Less than a generation later, Hawaiians, from toddlerhood through graduate school, can learn their ancestral language. At last count, the islands have no fewer than 18,400 native speakers of ʻŌlelo Hawaiʻi.

E hoʻi mai ʻoe (come back.)

Both Sanford B. Dole and Larry Kimura had more than an inkling of the role schools play in shaping society. To bring about the kind of educational change we need will take a substantial number of people with similar sophisticated understandings of *why* schools have such profound influence on society and *how* systems change. It will take a cadre of people who know that schools host and cultivate our "deepest…beliefs about how the world works" and replicate the way society collectively thinks generation after generation, no matter how obsolete that way of thinking has become or how inhumane it has always been. When my deep longing for *what* I know our schools could be rises within me, I feel tender and hopeful—like I did that morning at Pūnana Leo O Maui. But I also know that *why* and *how* we get to the *what* is much more akin to my squirmy flight home from Pittsburgh than it is to a perfect day in paradise.

Even so, I invite you to the journey. Buckle up.

2

How Paradigms Shift

Most of us have no idea of the assumptions
and beliefs we use to create our perceptions.
We think we're open-minded and curious when, in fact,
we all suffer from "paradigm blindness."
~ Dr. Margaret Wheatley

My oldest kids, George and Charissa, are twins. At age six, they started their public education journey at a brand-new neighborhood school near where we lived in Central Pennsylvania. On their first day of first grade, I left work early so I could be there when they got home. I pulled into our garage with a few minutes to spare. Hopping out of the minivan, I kicked off my pumps inside the back door and slipped on flats. I turned on the oven and grabbed prepackaged cookie dough and milk from the fridge. Just as I plopped the twelfth sticky lump on a cookie sheet, the school bus squealed to a stop at the top of the hill behind our house. I slid the cookies into the oven with a twinge of guilt. Not homemade, but still a special treat.

I went outside to greet them. Dusty green leaves edged in gold glimmered on the neighborhood trees as the late afternoon sun cast long shadows across the cul-de-sac. Children's voices spilled over the hill as small faces appeared at the crest. The twins walked toward me, waving goodbye to their friends. I smiled. My babies were growing up.

They waved off their last friend and turned toward home. When they saw me, their smiles vanished. They reached our driveway and stomped past me without even a glance in my direction. "How could you do that to us? We were so embarrassed!"

Visions of them gobbling down cookies amidst happy chatter evaporated. I'd planned this day so carefully. What did I get wrong?

Inside, they slipped their bright little backpacks off their shoulders and dropped them to the floor. They followed me into the kitchen. I pulled the cookies from the oven and began moving them to a plate as they scooched onto stools at the breakfast bar.

I waited, hoping the issue would show itself quickly. They did not disappoint.

"*What is the poem?*" they demanded. "Why didn't you *teach us the poem?*"

I froze, eyebrows furrowed, warm cookie on spatula suspended midair.

"Poem? What poem?"

George scoffed. "Mom, *you* don't know *the poem?*"

Charissa reached for the suspended cookie. "*All* the kids knew the poem, Mom. Every single one. We were the *only* ones that didn't."

I was flummoxed (or, in Pennsylvania Dutch, *ferhoodled*). What kind of mother was I, not knowing the all-important poem? Was this a Pennsylvania thing? In California, we had no poem that every first grader knew the first day of school. We had no poem that every child knew at any time of any year.

I continued offloading cookies. "Tell me more," I said. "What was the poem about?"

George swallowed a bite of cookie and chased it with milk. "First thing in the morning all the kids stood up and faced the front of the classroom."

Oh.

Oh no.

I suddenly saw it all. The kids. All standing. Facing the front of the classroom.

Even after seven years living in Pennsylvania Dutch country, I remained amused by my cultural gaffes.

I stifled a giggle.

Oblivious to my contorted face, George grabbed another cookie. "They put their hands on their chests and said the poem. A flag poem."

Oh. My. Goodness. I broke out a full-fledged cackle. *My* kid just called the Pledge of Allegiance a flag poem! Perfect! How else would an uninitiated six-year-old think of it?

And how could I have forgotten it?

Even with everything I had prepared for that day: their new shoes and haircuts, the backpacks and lunch boxes, rearranging my schedule, the milk and cookies, I had failed to give them *the* ticket in—how did I forget to teach them to pledge the flag?

It didn't matter that I checked my list twice; the pledge wasn't on it.

It also hadn't been in the curriculum. For preschool and kindergarten, George and Charissa attended a small community school run by a local group of (relatively) contemporary Mennonites, who didn't drive horse-drawn buggies or wear old-order clothes but still held fast to their convictions about the separation of church and state.

There were no flags of any kind in their schools. There was no flag poem.

George and Charissa were indignant. How could I laugh?

This would be a good place for me to pause and talk about the power of cultural symbolism or ponder how a few sentences can come to represent what it means to be patriotic. But in a chapter about paradigms, the most important thing about this story is how utterly I didn't see the flag poem coming. Without a thought, I assumed my kids learned to pledge the flag in school, just as I had been taught thirty years before. It didn't matter that I knew Mennonites wouldn't teach them. In my mind, schools, not parents, taught the pledge.

Paradigms, and the assumptions they create, do that to us. They keep us from seeing what would otherwise be obvious. When we do start to see what would otherwise be obvious, we squirm. We question assumptions we didn't even know we had. Like what is the moral and ethical considerations of pledging loyalty to a flag?

Or can I really own land?

Why the Prevailing Paradigm Matters

Paradigms shape society. They are to human thinking, individual and collective, what a potter is to clay. Dr. Angayuqaq Oscar Kawagley, the late Native Alaskan scholar and educator, saw paradigms, or as he called them, worldviews, as the heart of cultural identity. "Once a worldview has been formed, the people are then able to identify themselves as a unique people. The worldview enables its possessors to make sense of the world around them, make artifacts to fit their world, generate behavior, and interpret their experiences."

A society's worldview, or prevailing paradigm, generates its collective behavior and gives the lens through which its members interpret the world. Developing a clear-eyed understanding of our society's prevailing paradigm is key to understanding why we educate young humans the way we do and is central to creating a whole new way of doing school. Dr. Donella Meadows, quoted in the previous chapter, put it this way: "Whether it was Copernicus and Kepler showing that the earth is not the center of the universe, or Einstein hypothesizing that matter and energy are interchangeable,...people who have managed to intervene in systems at the level of paradigm have hit a leverage point that totally transforms systems."

It's easy to look down our modern noses at the fools of ancient history who took for granted that the sun and other planets circle Earth, but we are in the same position today as they were then. Our individual and collective Western perceptions, concepts, and habits of mind have been indelibly shaped by a powerful but now obsolete paradigm. Despite how obviously inaccurate the paradigm may be, for at least the last five hundred years Western society's worldview has imagined the universe and everything in it as a machine.

The solar system *is a machine.*

The Earth *is a machine.*

The human brain *is a machine.*

Where did we get this universe-as-machine idea? According to philosopher Dr. Mary Midgley, modern science grew up alongside the industrial revolution. "...The dominant symbol shaping all speculation about [science] was the vision of something that was then quite new—machinery.... The universe began to appear as a vast clock, and everything within it as a cog or a wheel in the clock's mechanism."

I am a scientist and I use machines every day. I am not against either. However, we have all been taught to stuff the awe-inspiring universe of nonmachine phenomena into mechanistic boxes without realizing that's what we're doing. The mechanistic view isn't recognized as just *one of many* ways of knowing, but instead, for centuries, it has been Western society's *only credible* way of knowing. We create systems and artifacts consistent with this only credible way of knowing, including the systems and artifacts of schooling (curricula, desks, pencils, school buildings, tests, teacher qualifications, content standards).

"No, no, no!" you may protest. "I don't see education as a machine! I certainly don't think of humans, especially children, as machines!" But if you Google images of educational systems, you'll find lightbulbs and schematics, gears and pulleys, and lots of boxes and arrows. The graphics depicting schools look far more like assembly lines and motherboards than a riparian ecosystem. Google "brain" and you'll find more gears, pulleys, and lightbulbs. Just today someone I deeply respect posted a social media meme saying our brains are "programmable." Information processing, a popular learning science theory, agrees.

As a society steeped in this mechanistic way of conceptualizing everything, we have become dangerously ignorant of the ways of thinking that can help us understand how the complex world works. With global complexity increasing exponentially, it is not hyperbole to say that continuing to raise humans to think primarily in mechanistic ways jeopardizes the future of humanity and the planet. Although living through paradigmatic change is always a bumpy ride, paradigmatic change is the path of true transformation.

We've also been taught in many subtle ways that we as ordinary individuals have very little power to influence societal change. But we do. Paradigmatic change often happens in the wake of a major event, but more often it happens when ordinary people, just like you and me, start to see things differently, start to act on what we see, and start to influence others. This book is about how you, my dear reader, can influence your world in such a way that an entirely new way of doing school emerges.

What Is a Paradigm?

First, we need the background on paradigms. The term *paradigm* was popularized by science philosopher Dr. Thomas Kuhn in his 1962 book *The Structure of Scientific Revolutions*. He used the term to refer to overarching concepts that organize *normal science*.

Normal science is status quo science.

It is science chugging along as expected, expanding on what is already known and not rocking any theoretical boats.

In the last six decades, the term paradigm has also been applied to the beliefs that make up a society's worldview. I use paradigm both ways: to refer to normal science, and synonymously with the term worldview. I use both terms to mean *organized sets of beliefs that so deeply guide a society (or body of scientific work) that the assumptions they generate are rarely questioned and almost always invisible.*

Societies structure themselves around paradigms and define themselves by the assumptions their paradigms generate. Paradigmatic assumptions form the invisible and unspoken framework that shape societies' institutions, including schools. They determine what people pay attention to and what goes unnoticed. In a massive, iterative process, paradigms generate the assumptions a society lives by, and those assumptions hold the paradigm in place.

Because of this interdependent, self-preserving, and self-replicating relationship, once established, paradigms run on autopilot. Assumptions such as those mentioned by Dr. Meadows, like thinking that nouns and verbs are different kinds of words or that one can own land but not air, operate so deeply it feels as if we know their logic, even though we rarely do. We are often only aware of societal assumptions when we inadvertently violate them, like if we fail to teach uninitiated first-graders the flag poem.

Pause for a moment and see if you can identify some of the unquestioned assumptions that show up in how we do school. I'm going to just spitball a few.

There are sets of facts, ideas, and skills that children should learn at certain ages.

Kids learn best from professional educators.

Grades mean something.

In educator circles we talk a lot about "evidence-based" practices, but if we're brutally honest, we know that every statement I listed above is based on assumptions and not empirical evidence. Paradigmatic assumptions, far more than research from learning or developmental sciences, keeps schools doing what they do, because that's the purpose of paradigmatic assumptions. Just as with normal science, in society paradigms define, structure, and fortify *the status quo*. They are relentlessly self-perpetuating. Paradigms are not about change. Paradigms define and defend "normal."

The assumptions that paradigms generate are neither good nor bad. They consolidate information and relieve our minds of clutter. They help people in a shared culture operate automatically from common values and priorities. Paradigmatic assumptions, however, also limit our thinking and narrow our perception of possibilities. This characteristic is often referred to as paradigm blindness. Even the most open-minded among us are paradigm blind.

Is Girl Scouts Real?

We often don't see that our assumptions about others are always incomplete and often inaccurate. They can also keep us from seeing potential in ourselves. I had a front-row seat to this dynamic a few years ago as I led a community-based project funded by the National Science Foundation. Our team held a STEM learning day focused on engaging young girls who lived in a San Diego neighborhood.

Sylvia Acevedo, then CEO of Girl Scouts USA, accepted my invitation to come to San Diego and share her story. Sylvia grew up in a migrant farm community. Being a Girl Scout from a young age gave her the confidence and skills to become a rocket scientist. After college, she joined Jet Propulsion Laboratories as one of their first Latina engineers and helped design NASA rockets.

On our community engagement day, Sylvia and I headed to the elementary school in Southeastern San Diego where the project was based. Happy voices spilled out from the multipurpose room as we made our way over from the school office. The front of the room was set up for an assembly. In the back, over a hundred girls gathered around long cafeteria tables strewn with colorful supplies. All the children were Latinas. A half-dozen Girl Scout staff worked alongside teachers, guiding the girls through real-life science activities like those they could do to earn Girl Scout badges.

Sylvia and I, along with several community leaders, made our way around the room, marveling at all the girls were doing. Then Sylvia moved to the front of the room and the girls took their seats. As she talked about growing up in New Mexico, you could almost smell the tamales and see the fields ready for harvest. Sylvia switched easily between English and Spanish, evoking giggles and knowing nods from teachers and students alike.

I stood toward the back. Eric, an influential nonprofit executive walked over and stood next to me. Weeks earlier I had visited Eric to seek his help with funding scout troops at the school. He had listened, then explained that I should never have positioned the project where I did. He told me the community was too entrenched in generational poverty to benefit from my efforts. He quoted stats on the low rates at which Latinas enter scientific fields and said the local Girl Scout council had tried recruiting at the school but there was no interest.

I was wasting my time and an NSF grant.

At a loss for a professional response, I had taken a deep breath and invited him to come see for himself. Three weeks later, we stood side by side as Sylvia wrapped up and invited the girls to ask questions. Dozens of hands flew up. Sylvia pointed to a student. "Yes?" she asked.

A girl stood, took the microphone a teacher offered, and asked, "Is Girl Scouts *real*?"

Sylvia stared at the girl. Then she looked at me.

I shrugged. I had no clue what the girl meant.

Sylvia looked back to the child. "Could you repeat your question?"

The girl nodded. "Is Girl Scouts *real*?"

Sylvia looked at me again.

I was about to shrug again when I remembered that a performance art company had visited the school a few weeks before and invited students to participate in an improvised play. Was the girl asking if Girl Scouts is performance art? Was she asking if the science activities were mere props, and the students were just pretending? Before I could clarify, the girl did so herself.

"Is this just a play? Or is it *real*? Like, could I be a Girl Scout?"

Another child stood up. "Are you going away and never coming back? Or can we do Girl Scouts again tomorrow?"

The room erupted as the girls clapped out a cadence.

"Girl Scouts tomorrow! Do Girl Scouts tomorrow!"

Sylvia laughed and clapped along. Then she stood directly in front of the girl with the microphone. "Yes. Girl Scouts is *real*, and yes, *you* can be a Girl Scout." She waved her arm as if taking in the whole room. "You can *all* be Girl Scouts!"

I glanced sideways to see Eric dabbing his eyes. He wasn't the only one who held assumptions that limited his perspective of the children in that room. The girls had their own. Until that day, to them Girl Scouts was just as likely fantasy as fact. They had never gone with a parent to drop off a sibling at Brownies. They had never sold cookies or gone on a scout camping trip. Their opportunities to see themselves as scientists were shaped by assumptions outside their control. But the girl who stood up and reached for a microphone that day did something different than the executive standing at my side: she took it upon herself to question her assumptions.

She sought disconfirming information.

She wondered, aloud, in front of everyone, if perhaps, just maybe, things were different than what she had assumed: *Could I be a Girl Scout?*

At its core, Sylvia's story is about how Girl Scouts shaped her self-perceptions before societal assumptions could disfigure them. Her story helped the young Latinas in that room take a well-aimed swing at assumptions of limited potential about themselves and their community.

All of us who were raised in schools as we know them have a disfigured understanding about what learning is and what school could be. In this book, I invite you to seek disconfirming information, to wonder aloud, perhaps in front of everyone, if maybe things could be different than what we assume, like *can we have inclusive, diverse, humane, and regenerative schools*?

Yes, we can.

How Paradigms Shape Society

Paradigms and their assumptions seep into daily life and shape the ways we collectively live via mental models. Mental models are metaphors, images, scripts, rules, scenes, routines, and ways of reasoning that give concrete meaning to abstract ideas. They organize the assumptions generated by society's paradigms into beliefs that seem real and unquestionably true, like nouns and verbs are different types of words.

Or the purpose of schools is to populate the workforce pipeline.

Or children's brains are systems of gears and pulleys, or worse, programmable.

Mental models help us simplify complexity by making patterns easier to spot and routines easier to follow. Without them we couldn't effectively navigate our complex world. We have mental models for everything from who and what is safe or not, to how to navigate restaurants and airports, to where food comes from. We have mental models for how to behave when people stand, turn toward a flag, and put their hands over their hearts. People are so adept at following mental models that most six-year-old humans in the United States readily recite the flag poem on their first day of school with no thought to its significance.

As we will see in this and the following chapters, the prevailing machine paradigm shows up in innumerable ways in everyday life in Western schools. The metaphors, images, rules, routines, and even the structure of the school day and the way most school buildings and classrooms are designed communicates the assumptions and expectations of the prevailing machine paradigm.

How Paradigms Shift

Most people who care about paradigms aren't all that interested in the status quo. Most are interested in how paradigms change and are particularly interested in disruption, which some folks (particularly in the business sector) erroneously equate with innovation. Disruption is seen as bold! Even sexy. But, as we shall see in later chapters, ill-placed or ill-timed disruption is a great way to strengthen the status quo, not dislodge it. Paradigm-shifting disruption is part of a *process*. Understanding that process is essential to being effective changemakers. Paradigms shift in phases:

- Phase 1: Normal
- Phase 2: Huh?
- Phase 3: Aha!
- Phase 4: New Normal

Interestingly, the ways humans learn and the ways paradigms shift are so remarkably similar that we can learn how paradigms shift by considering something a bit more ordinary, like how a young child learns about animals. Let's imagine a toddler I'll call Aisha and her family, which includes a caring uncle and a dog.

Phase 1: Normal

For several weeks, Aisha thrilled her loved ones by repeating the word "dog" whenever she sees the family's pup. Aisha started saying "dog" while petting their pooch, leading her delighted parents to assume Aisha "knows" what a dog is.

Then the family visits a zoo and Aisha sees an elephant. Aisha has never seen an elephant before. Seeing something that is like her pet, albeit somewhat different, she points to the elephant and exclaims, "dog!"

Her parents are perplexed. Did Aisha forget what a dog is?

No, she didn't. This is the *Normal* phase. It is exactly what status quo does. Whether it is status quo about the sun circling Earth, or status quo about what a toddler calls a four-legged creature, or status quo about how we do school, in the Normal phase, encountering something different rarely makes a difference. At least not at first. Aisha's status quo mental model of "dog" emphasizes and incorporates everything about the elephant that resembles a dog and ignores as irrelevant whatever does not.

Size? Irrelevant.

Long nose? Irrelevant.

Four legs? Integrated into existing dog mental model.

Aisha perceived an animal that is substantively different from her mental model for "dog," but the differences she saw did not make a difference. No new learning happened. Her mental model of "dog" includes the beast before her, differences be damned.

This is how the Normal phase works in science too. According to Kuhn, when status quo science encounters new information it does one of two things: it assimilates it or dismisses it. This is how the belief that the sun moves around Earth persisted for so long even after compelling evidence showed the model was wrong. Societies do this too. They assimilate or dismiss. Differences, at least at first, do not make a difference. This is why schools remain the same despite decades of evidence that schools no longer meet society's needs.

If Aisha's mental model of "elephant" does not encounter differences that make it impossible to assimilate or dismiss, to her, elephants and dogs will remain conceptually the same. Her understanding of animals will remain immature. When differences that could make a difference and bring about more complex understandings (for a toddler or a society) get absorbed into the status quo, the unique features of the differences simply disappear.

When contradictory facts challenge paradigms, the go-to response, for both individuals and societies, is to assimilate or ignore the differences and perpetuate the status quo. Thus, most people shrug at strip mining or extracting fossil fuels from ancient layers of stored carbon because any evidence that Earth is alive is assimilated into existing mental models of our planet as machine.

Few people flinch when human brains are described as the most powerful information processor on the planet. Despite breathtaking functional magnetic resonance imaging (fMRI) that shows brain functions are massively complex self-organizing organic processes, thinking and cognition—even children's cognition—are frequently depicted as machines. Google "cognition" and select "images" to see what I mean. The astounding nuances of fMRI images have been absorbed into the mental models generated by the prevailing paradigm: brains are systems of pulleys, cogs, and gears.

The famed Swiss biologist and developmental theorist Dr. Jean Piaget called the process of absorbing new information *assimilation*. When ethnic and cultural differences are absorbed by a dominant culture, that's also assimilation. Differences that could contribute to rich, complex, and nuanced societal learning disappear.

You will save yourself mountains of grief if you understand the power of the Normal phase. In the story about Girl Scouts, as belittling as Eric's statements were about the community where I worked, my appreciation for the Normal phase is why I took a deep breath, kept my arguments to myself, and invited him to hear Sylvia. My words didn't stand a chance against his status quo assumptions, but his *experiences* in that school auditorium just might. I had no idea what would happen that day, but I invited him into the *container* for that day to experience whatever would happen.

When society or individuals either assimilate or ignore disconfirming information, *no new learning occurs*. Unless the Normal phase enters a robust Huh? phase, status quo carries on indefinitely. Few people are as brave as the child who stood and publicly asked if Girl Scouts is real. Few people intentionally seek information that challenges their assumptions. One of the primary jobs of an effective paradigmatic change agent is to set conditions for people to encounter differences that challenge the assumptions of the Normal phase, including our own assumptions. Setting conditions, inviting people into experiences, and being intentional about how we consider and use containers are some of the practical skills and practices we'll explore in depth in later chapters.

Phase 2: Huh?

Piaget called the Huh? phase disequilibrium. Thomas Kuhn called it disruption. It's the phase when we start to question that which was assumed to be unquestionable. Huh? tells us something is off and warrants our attention. Huh? doesn't happen linearly or predictably. It is a process, not a singular (disruptive) event.

Huh? can feel threatening, and in many regards, it is. Huh? tells us we have encountered information that we can't easily assimilate. For a human, that's disconcerting. We all prefer the familiar safety of status quo. But disruption brings the status quo into the full illumination of disconfirming information. To truly grasp what happens in Huh? we need a deeper understanding of what information actually is.

Western education taught us to think about information as having meaning all on its own. It's code or data. A printout. Numbers or words. Books or articles. The World Wide Web is full of information, as are the famed reading rooms of Oxford University Library or the US Library of Congress.

Or are they?

The late anthropologist and complexity scientist Dr. Gregory Bateson famously defined information as *a difference that makes a difference*. If you go back and read the section on the Normal phase again, you'll see I repeatedly refer to differences that *didn't* make a difference. In the complexity sciences, that means those differences were not information. That's a fundamentally different way of thinking about information than what most of us have been taught. In Bateson's definition, information isn't information because it exists. Information is information because it has an effect. Information *makes a difference*. If the words in a dusty tome on an Oxford shelf haven't made a difference in three hundred years, is it information? Are data buried on the Internet where no one can find or use them information?

According to Bateson, no.

So, "information" that gets assimilated into the status quo is also not information.

I realize this point might seem a bit too deep into the theoretical weeds, but understanding this point strikes at the core of how very different, how very useful, joyful, and productive our schools could (and should) be. When schools teach inert, inactive information, no learning happens. Whatever does go on is, well, dead, whereas authentic learning is teeming with life. We're going to talk about the relationship between life and learning in Chapter 4, but it's important to understand at this point that the reason we need *regenerative* learning in our schools is because the majority of what we've come to assume is "education" isn't learning at all. Regenerative learning breathes life back into school, and one of the critical ways it does that is by embracing and using differences (lots more on this idea throughout the book).

Let's get back to our toddler at the zoo. Imagine that when Aisha says "dog" and points to the elephant, her uncle kneels next to her and says, "No, it's not a dog. That's an elephant. See, it is much bigger than a dog. It has very big ears. Its long nose is called a trunk. It uses its trunk to eat and spray water."

Don't get ahead of yourself here.

No, Aisha does not smile sweetly and exclaim, "Elephant!"

Typically, when a cherished idea is challenged, young children (or an entire society) will scrunch their face, plant a foot firmly on the ground, point at the elephant and say, "DOG!" That's exactly what Aisha did, telling her uncle in no uncertain terms that the massive gray thing was, in fact, a DOG!

Differences that make a difference start the Huh? phase, and without Huh? there is no new learning. There is only status quo. But starting Huh? is not enough. No Huh? process successfully ends with an enlightened Aha! without first going through pushback. Aisha's uncle focused her attention on the differences between an elephant and a dog, making those differences difficult to ignore. When humans, as individuals or as a society, encounter a real live Huh? our instinct is to end the discomfort quickly via assimilation, but when faced with differences that make assimilation impossible, humans (and human systems) push back, hard.

Pushback is not a separate phase. Pushback is an essential part of Huh? and serves a critical function. Pushback vets the new information, questioning its veracity, testing it to see if it makes more sense than the status quo. New paradigms do not emerge from disruption that merely ruffles feathers. Paradigm shifts don't come about when a pebble ripples a pond. Disruption is about individual minds and the mind of society completely reorganizing around new, solidly vetted, and impossible-to-disregard information. The shift doesn't come about from a little "Oh, I hadn't known that before" epiphany. Paradigm shifts are full-on reorganizations of what we all assumed, without a second thought, to be true and real. Like, you know, nouns and verbs might not be different kinds of words and maybe it isn't possible to own land.

Being an educational changemaker means we courageously focus on differences that make a difference and make those differences impossible to ignore. But we also ensure we have a rock solid understanding of the new paradigm from which we speak. This book is a guide to the change process, but in it I also propose a new societal paradigm—regeneration. I propose a way of thinking and living that is different in nearly all ways from the machine paradigm. Successfully focusing attention on the differences between these paradigms takes more than courage; it also takes finesse. We know that spotlighting differences between the machine-based status quo and ideas that challenge it will not lead to the prevailing paradigm rolling over and wagging its tail. Wise changemakers know that when mounting evidence challenges a society-defining paradigm, the society will do all it can to preserve it. Savvy changemakers are ready for the pushback and know when, why, how, and how much to engage.

They are also relentlessly patient.

As is Aisha's family. Although it's wise to continue to call an elephant an elephant, there's no need to provoke a battle of wills with a two-year-old at the zoo. Better to move on to another elephant and highlight the differences again, speaking with full assurance that the animal in the exhibit is, indeed, an elephant. The child will likely call it a dog. That's okay. Move to the giraffes. And the lions. When leaving the zoo, stop by the gift shop and pick up a picture book about zoo animals and read it often.

Keep coming back to the Huh? phase.

With repeated exposure to differences that disconfirm the idea that all four-legged creatures are a dog Aisha will eventually "get it" and her mental model will shift. It might not shift completely or completely accurately, but it will shift enough to form a new conceptual understanding about the diversity of four-legged creatures.

The Huh? phase can be turbulent and consume enormous resources. Changemakers who understand complexity only set conditions for disruption when it is clearly strategic and when there are enough resources at the ready to withstand pushback. If not, the prevailing paradigm becomes even stronger. It's the same reason you don't stop taking an antibiotic while a bacterial infection rages in your lungs. Doing so will make the infection come back even stronger. We'll explore disruption further in Chapter 10, "How Systems Learn." For now, know that forcing disruption for disruption's sake is more than ill-advised, it's counterproductive.

Effective educational changemakers understand disruption as a complex volatile phenomenon that presents a quandary. If the only way to unseat a paradigm is to come at it loudly and often with disconfirming information, what do you do when the system inevitably pushes back?

You expect it. You plan for it. You prepare yourself.

Once prepared and engaged, you never give up. You keep coming back.

You are unrelenting and strategic, speaking with the full assurance from the new paradigm. Eventually, the system hits a tipping point and there is no turning back.

Phase 3: Aha!

You don't get to Aha! by merely accumulating a sufficient amount of information. Aha! happens via *reorganization*. For Aisha to form a proper understanding of "elephant," she must reorganize the concepts "dog," "elephant," and "animal" into new relationships. For Aisha, "dog" must shift to being a concept representing one of many four-legged beings, not a catchall for them all. It also moves to being a subcategory of the more abstract notion of "animal." If you are like me and you read with a highlighter in hand, whip it out now and highlight *reorganization* and *relationships*. Those two ideas are at the heart of both authentic learning (versus memorization) and paradigm shifts. We'll revisit them in future chapters.

Reorganizing relationships between ideas or concepts is why getting to Aha! is hard. It's like when you buy decorations on sale the day after a holiday. You get them home, but there isn't a convenient place to store them. You could reorganize your garage, but you're tired. So instead you toss your purchases out of the way on a high empty shelf where they're forgotten. When the season rolls around again, they're out of sight and you don't even remember buying them, so your decorations look the same as last year. That's assimilation. Things were not reorganized in a way that made the new decorations accessible and useful. Your decorations didn't change. They didn't make it to the Aha! phase.

A paradigm shift is a tipping point at which a society can no longer function adequately without reorganizing its fundamental assumptions about the world around new, undeniable information. New information (differences that make a difference) overwhelms the existing paradigm beyond the point of no return and society reorganizes the mental models it lives by.

Paradigm shifts are massive and profound, but they do not change reality. Rather, they reorganize our *perceptions* of reality. We do not change the way the world works. Paradigms are *perceptions* of the way the world works. They are organized worldviews that a culture accepts and allows nonconsciously to shape society. When society shifted from an Earth-centered to a sun-centered paradigm, the sun, Earth, and other planets stayed their course. Paradigm shifts reorganize the worldview, but how the world works stays the same.

Reconfigured understanding of reality can yield profound differences in how humans live. The Earth-centered to sun-centered shift showed up not only in new models of planetary bodies but in revised understanding about humanity's place in the universe. Our collective understanding shifted from a universe with humans at the center to humans inhabiting one among many planets in similar orbits around the sun.

In a fascinating similarity to human development, children begin life in what developmental psychologists call egocentrism: young children perceive themselves as the center of their world. As children explore and engage with more complexity, their understanding of their place in the universe shifts. They start to see other perspectives and grow up into an understanding that their view is merely one among many. Seen this way, shifting paradigms, as turbulent as they may seem, can be understood as a maturational process, an evolution, if you will, from less complex to more complex understandings of reality.

Phase 4: New Normal

In the early 2000s, I was a casualty of a statewide educator layoff in California. Wanting to stay close to my aging mother in San Diego, I applied for jobs across Arizona and was offered a position in Tucson. Leaving the kids with my mom in San Diego, I traveled to Tucson to finalize my employment and find a home. I stayed for a few days at a jewel of a hotel in the Santa Catalina Mountains. With a major move a few weeks away, I figured an extra day to rest would do me good, and since I was visiting at the height of the Sonoran Desert summer, the room rate at this fabulous hotel was dirt cheap.

On my last night before heading home to the single-mom-about-to-move gig, having successfully rented a house and negotiated a higher salary, I treated myself to a thick novel and dinner salad in my room. Later that evening, as I turned off the lights, I realized I hadn't put my dinner tray outside and the remaining vinaigrette was smelly. I scampered out of bed wearing only a tushy-length nightie and grabbed the tray. Balancing it in one hand, I swung open the heavy hotel room door, planted my right heel firmly against it, stepped forward on my left foot, and bent over to set the tray on the floor.

And just like that it happened.

When I shifted my weight to bend over, the door, as if flung by a hurricane, swung closed. Whoosh! Out into the hallway I went, baby doll jammies and all. I froze, still holding the tray. I was no longer in my room. One second I was, and then, wham, with just a teensy shift, I was suddenly in a very different and disorienting place.

I surveyed my circumstance. I was nearly bare-bottomed and completely empty-handed (save for the smelly tray). No room key. No phone. No ID. My dignity silently crept away. Down the hallway, a man and a woman approached, gently laughing as they walked toward me. I put down the tray, hid as much of my nearly naked self as I could behind a pillar, and pretend-talked on a pretend phone—as if talking nearly naked outside at 11 p.m. was absolutely normal. Note, when we're immersed in a disorienting New Normal, pretending all is normal is, well, normal.

With the laughing duo safely out of sight, I tiptoed to an inside hallway where, thankfully, I found a house phone. The front desk clerk told me to come to the lobby for a key.

Um...no can do. You see...um...I'm not appropriately attired.

Ah. She understood. Ten of the longest minutes of my life later, a tall young security guard walked down the hall, nodding and chuckling.

"Well, you sure are in a predicament, aren't you?" he said.

This is what New Normal feels like. New Normal follows the Aha! that resolves the tension of Huh? But New Normal also feels like waking up in an entirely new place where the rules and resources are unknown and you feel nearly if not completely naked, alone, and out of place.

It's enticing to romanticize paradigm shifts. To see them as the blissful birth of whatever new thing we want to bring about. But like all births, paradigm shifts are messy. The remnants of the existing paradigm stay active for a long time. When a regenerative paradigm emerges, it doesn't mean machines or machine thinking will disappear. It means that individually and collectively we reconfigure the relationships between humans, the human-designed environment, and the natural world. Instead of seeing ecosystems as subject to the demands of the built environment, we expect buildings to revive and contribute to healthy ecosystems. Instead of seeing young humans as widgets destined for the workforce pipeline, we see them as the unique, sacred expressions of life that they are. We embrace our obligation to set conditions conducive to their lives and to all life, and teach them how to do the same.

That's an entirely different reason for schools to exist.

If you're like me, it's hard to imagine a society based on the assumption that mutual thriving is valued above all else. But then I remember how powerful a reorganizational Aha! is. When Aisha truly gets that there are lots and lots of very different four-legged creatures, when she reorganizes her understanding of how they are all related to each other and to her, she will explode with new realizations. She will never think of the family dog the same way again.

Paradigms Lost: Where Are We in the Shift?

As I'm writing, living in a regenerative society seems like a pipe dream. Never have so many people been trained so completely in the machine-based paradigm. With more than 90 percent of young humans growing up in the Western world spending the first twelve to eighteen years of their lives in experiences shaped by the machine-based paradigm, bumping that mechanistic Normal into Huh? seems impossible.

Still, throughout human history we have reorganized our collective worldview even without instant access to ideas and people around the globe. People on every continent recognize the machine paradigm has failed to bring about the widespread prosperity promised by industrialists. It enriched a wealthy few while depleting Earth's resources, putting all life at risk.

Given the immense inadequacies of the prevailing paradigm, it is no surprise that the signs of a societal shift are everywhere. When paradigm-challenging information becomes too much to ignore and the system pushes back, signaling the start of the disruptive phase, the new paradigm must be more than merely contradictory: it must be generative. It must generate a cohesive new paradigm that not only exposes the existing paradigm as inadequate but offers something much better.

The new paradigm that ultimately emerges will do so when it makes a paradigm-shifting difference. The difference that will make that kind of difference is our way of thinking.

3

A Whole New Way of Thinking

We cannot solve the problems of our time
with the same thinking that created them.
~ Dr. Albert Einstein

Our schools are, in a sense, factories, in which the raw
products (children) are to be shaped and fashioned into
products to meet the various demands of life.
The specifications for manufacturing come from the
demands of twentieth-century civilization, and it is
the business of the school to build its pupils
according to the specifications laid down.
~ Dr. Ellwood Patterson Cubberley

The sun rose round and yellow, warming the damp Pacific air as the *Fifth Lucky Dragon* swayed in the swells near Midway Atoll. The Japanese tuna boat's twenty-three-member crew hoisted their last net, empty and torn, like all the others that morning. They had yet to catch a single fish. The crew weighed anchor as the captain set a course for the Marshall Islands, a small Micronesian country of horseshoe-shaped atolls. Maybe their luck would turn.

The sun made its way up the sky from the eastern horizon, glimmering across the deep blue water as the crew dropped their nets ninety miles east of Bikini Atoll. In short order, they were hauling in tuna and reef sharks flapping wildly against their fate.

Like the unsuspecting fish, the crew of the *Fifth Lucky Dragon* went about their day unaware of what was about to befall them. As they processed their catch, a massive fireball exploded in the western sky, sending an ear-shattering roar rolling across the sea.

Frightened, the crew worked furiously, hauling in the burgeoning nets. They hastily processed the fish as a strange gray cloud crept toward them. Within minutes, gritty ash fell on catch and crew, sticking to flesh, fish, and clothing, and finding its way into eyes, ears, gills, nostrils, and mouths. Barehanded, the crew brushed debris off their catch, unaware it was radioactive sand and coral that had been blasted three hundred feet skyward from Bikini Atoll.

Six hours later, when they set off for their home port, the crew's skin was raw and blistered. Most were vomiting and sick with headache and diarrhea. By the time they arrived home two weeks later, all had symptoms of acute radiation syndrome. All were hospitalized for over a year. Two of the crew died within six months.

The fireball that lit up the Pacific sky was Castle Bravo, a fifteen-megaton hydrogen bomb brainchild of nuclear physicists at the Los Alamos Scientific Laboratory and Operations Crossroads in New Mexico. Castle Bravo, a project of the secret US thermo-nuclear weapons testing program based in the Marshall Islands was designed to release a five to six megaton payload. That morning, it inadvertently delivered over two-and-a-half times that force, enough to obliterate any major city on Earth in a fraction of a second.

The crew of the *Fifth Lucky Dragon* were not the only victims. US military commanders detonated Castle Bravo despite warnings from meteorologists that the trade winds had shifted overnight, putting populated Marshall Islands atolls in the direct path of the nuclear fallout. That morning, the huge ash cloud rained nuclear waste on entire Marshallese villages. Seventy years later, the sea, the land, and the people have yet to recover.

We Have to Learn to Think in a New Way

Eighteen months after Castle Bravo obliterated Bikini Atoll, and half a globe away, a white-haired man in a black suit stepped forward in a dark conference room, taking his place before an assortment of stout microphones clustered atop a heavy wooden table. Bertrand Russell adjusted his wire-rimmed glasses, unfolded a small stack of papers, and began reading *Notice to the World*, a manifesto he had co-authored with Albert Einstein, who had died a few months earlier.

> "...We shall try to say no single word which should appeal to one group rather than to another. All, equally, are in peril, and, if the peril is understood, there is hope that they may collectively avert it.
>
> We have to learn to think in a new way.
>
> ...A bomb can now be manufactured which will be 2,500 times as powerful as that which destroyed Hiroshima. Such a bomb...sends radioactive particles into the upper air. They sink gradually and reach the surface of the earth in the form of a deadly dust.... It was this dust which infected the Japanese fishermen and their catch of fish. No one knows how widely such lethal radio-active particles might be diffused, but the best authorities are unanimous in saying that a war with H-bombs might possibly put an end to the human race."

Living and Learning in a Complex, Globally Connected World

Over the last several decades, the world and its problems have grown exponentially more complex than what Einstein and Russell decried in their treatise. Nuclear annihilation remains an existential threat. In addition, the climate crisis is nearing an irreversible tipping point, and grotesque economic inequities continue to widen.

These global problems emerged from our current ways of thinking.

Our current ways of thinking cannot fix them.

Even with the growing urgency, we still have not learned to think in a new way. We live with a collective false sense of security, trusting in our modern-day marvels, believing our educated masses are immune to the perils of previous generations. Yet, despite knowing that in the very recent past huge populations of First Nations and Indigenous peoples were wiped out by viruses imported by European colonizers, even the most technologically advanced nations were caught unprepared by the COVID-19 pandemic.

COVID-19 awakened us to just how connected our world is and what that interconnectedness means for daily life. Prepandemic, we were hardly impressed when people flew nonstop from Sydney to New York. We shrugged off worries when Wall Street jitters rattled markets in Beijing. We took as normal that throw pillows sold on Amazon were designed in Italy and made in Vietnam with Australian wool. We ordered them on our phones, choosing two-day delivery, not thinking about how the global connectedness that made that purchase possible might disrupt our lives.

That naivety is gone. We now know a microbe can jump species half a world away, show up in our local grocery, kill millions in mere months, shut down schools, overwhelm state-of-the-science medical systems, and thrust unemployment into the depression-era stratosphere.

COVID-19 set most heads spinning, but not everyone was surprised. While global connectivity inched its way into every societal cranny, some professions paid attention. It was their job to pay attention. For decades, epidemiologists, cybersecurity experts, military strategists, and data scientists, among others, have studied how complexity behaves when increasing numbers of people interact in an increasing number of ways. Certainly, economists and biologists have reason to study complexity, but it hasn't been at all clear what complexity science has to do with schools.

Until COVID-19.

In March 2020, the global dynamics that delivered pillows to our porches landed squarely in the laps of superintendents, teachers, parents, and workers in every organization that interfaces with or depends on education as we know it. With few exceptions, the impact of COVID-19 caught school systems, from early learning through higher education, completely off-guard, leaving teachers scrambling to craft Zoom-friendly lessons while delivering classes with unfamiliar software. Parents-turned-crisis-homeschoolers donned brave faces for what was supposed to be a two-week stint.

As weeks turned into months and as proms and commencements were canceled, parents posted Facebook memes of throwing back whiskey by nine a.m. while promising to never again vote down a teacher raise.

The New Normal

To ease our angst, we like to think the COVID-19 pandemic, and the accompanying educational havoc, was an anomaly. As we bared our arms and got our vaccinations (and hoped others would too), we soothed ourselves with talk of getting "back to normal" when "this is over."

But the complexity we are in will never be over.

The COVID-19 pandemic was not an anomaly.

Global complexity, and its attendant impacts, has been the new normal for quite some time. As the Omicron variant eased up in the United States, China was shutting down major cities which worsened global supply chain difficulties, and Russia attacked Ukraine, keeping the global economy and relations between countries uncertain and unstable. As the pandemic eased and supply chains recovered, all hell broke loose in the Middle East.

In this new normal, we learned something: education can happen in ways no one previously thought it could. Kids *can* learn from home as well as in a classroom, schedules *can* be flexible, pickup basketball in a corner lot or yoga with the dog in the living room *can* count as phys ed. But as health restrictions eased and schools reopened, rather than incorporating this new flexibility, schools ditched most adaptations and snapped back to rigid conformity. One parent of a high school sophomore told me, "My son has had all kinds of freedom you normally don't have at his age. He can go out in the neighborhood, go into town, in the middle of the day. Next year they're all going back in."

Back in.

Back into what? To a system far removed from the complex reality of everyday human life and from the new ways of thinking Einstein and Russel begged us to learn more than sixty-five years ago.

Education as we know it was not designed for this new normal.

It was never intended to prepare children for living in this level of global complexity.

As Dr. Margaret Wheatley writes in *Leadership and the New Science*, "We try hard to respond to these challenges and threats through our governments, organizations, and as individuals, but our actions fail us. No matter what we do, stability and lasting solutions elude us. It's time to realize that we will never cope with this new world using our old maps. It is our fundamental way of interpreting the world—our worldview—that must change."

We must learn to think in a new way.

Complexity and Complication

A paradigm shift will only happen when enough people have shifted their own thinking so they can amplify differences that make a difference. In later chapters, you will learn a method for identifying where (containers), what (differences), and how (exchanges) to effectively set conditions for society shifting to a regenerative paradigm. Before we get there, we need to work on our own mental models about how the world works and explore one of the most important distinctions of our time: the difference between complexity and complication.

Although the terms are often used interchangeably, complication is not complexity; complexity is not complication.

Stay with me here. This chapter is intended to bump you into the Huh? phase.

I'm going to introduce a good deal of theory. But as the late organizational psychologist Dr. Kurt Lewin famously said, there is nothing as practical as good theory. I encourage you to read this chapter slowly. Let it soak in. Wrestle with your questions and skepticism, just like I did on that plane ride home from Pittsburgh, and accept skepticism for what it is: normal pushback. Ask it to take a nap in a comfy chair while you explore these ideas. I promise, once you begin to see complexity and complication as distinct yet interacting phenomena, you will never look at the world or how it works the same way again.

When I first heard a complexity scientist differentiate complexity from complication, I thought she was splitting semantic hairs. Why make a big deal out of what seems to be essentially the same thing? But as I learned more, I began to see that although complexity and complication might seem similar on their surface, they are fundamentally different. I came to see that I was missing a powerful way of seeing the world—a way of thinking that was entirely new to me but as ancient as the universe.

I also realized that not being able to see and work with complexity is the critical problem with education as we know it. Essentially, we have a system that uses *complication* to support a fundamentally *complex* human capacity: learning. Once we grasp just how complex learning is, we are well on our way to envisioning regenerative schools and how to create them.

A rudimentary way to think about the difference between complication and complexity is that complication has to do with what we humans create. Buildings are complicated. So are highways. Your coffeemaker is complicated. So is the laptop I'm using. Tax and building codes are complicated. So are calendars and clocks. We do see some complication outside of human enterprise. One could argue that beaver dams are complicated.

But for the most part, complication refers to human-created objects, social structures, and machinery.

For the most part, although this is changing, complexity belongs to nature. All weather patterns are complex. Plants and animals are too. Brains and thinking are complex. Rivers, mountains, oceans, coral reefs, tides, and the solar system are all complex. In many ways, complicated things are humanity's way of dealing with, and, more often than not, attempting to control complexity.

Even though we are, and we live in, layers of connected complex systems, industrial era schools taught us to think almost exclusively in complication. Complexity thinking is essential for understanding the increasingly complex dynamics shaping our world, but schools do not teach students how to think in complexity. The prevailing machine paradigm, of necessity, obscures complexity. When we use our school-taught mechanistic thinking to act in highly complex situations, we become overwhelmed. There's too much information and too many considerations coming at us too fast, so we freeze. Or worse, we swirl, using lots of energy going nowhere fast. It's a full circle of yeah-buts. Examples abound: homelessness, affordable childcare, gun violence. When we solve one part of a complex problem with complicated means, it causes a problem elsewhere. So, we yeah-but that solution while someone presents a solution that solves their issue but causes a problem for someone else. And on it goes.

Eventually, a decision must be made, so knowing (or often not knowing) the scope of potential consequences someone (a parent, principal, president, program officer, police officer) breaks the paralysis, makes decisions, and holds their breath knowing somewhere, sometime in the foreseeable future, the dreaded Unintended Consequences *will* appear. Maybe the decision-maker will have moved on from their job by the time Unintended Consequences hit, and their successor will be left with the mop-up.

Unintended Consequences are the inevitable outcome of using reductionist problem-solving in complex situations. Complexity thinking doesn't magically predict all possible Unintended Consequences, but it helps us see far more of them in advance, helps us act in ways that mitigate those consequences, and, most importantly, helps us prepare for dealing with them effectively. Barreling into complex situations equipped with only reductionist thinking pretty much guarantees Unintended Consequences will be stronger and last longer, and make mitigation far more difficult, potentially impossible.

A regenerative paradigm is rooted in complexity. The machine paradigm is rooted in complication, as is our current education system. This doesn't mean that there is no complication in regenerative systems or complexity in reductionist machine-based systems. But it does mean that even folks who are adamantly committed to a whole new regenerative way of living and learning have been schooled from a young age to see the world in complicated terms. We can address this foundational problem by wrapping our heads around these two types of phenomena, how they differ, how they behave, and how we can influence both.

In this chapter, I separate complication and complexity to make a clear distinction, but in real life, they coexist and interact, often in ways that are hard to tease apart. Interstate freeway systems are complicated, as are the cars moving on them. But drivers, weather, fuel supply chains, and traffic are complex. Let's start with complication.

It's Complicated

When we think systems, most of us think of machines. We imagine gears, pulleys, structures, and assembly lines. All of that is complication. Machines, or complicated systems, have well-defined parts that interact in fixed and predictable ways, governed by a (usually large) set of complicated rules.

Layers and layers of rules.

Think of all the rules that govern how the parts of your car work. Or tax rules. Or the International Building Code. This is the stuff of factories, logic models, government regulations, grant requirements, and statistics.

It is, pun intended, complicated.

Complicated thinking works well in systems that have tight causes and effects among their parts—systems that are made up of things that are close to each other in time and space, especially those that we can easily see, control, and predict. When we step on the brake pedal, our car stops. When we flip a switch, a light turns on. We're used to these tight relationships. They're all around us, seem normal, and help us feel in control. They're often strung together in a sequence of smaller causes and effects that produce something we want. When I bake a loaf of bread, I control the ingredients and the procedures. Using a tried-and-true recipe gives me greater predictability. In each step, I do something and get an outcome. Knead for two minutes, the dough becomes elastic. Let it rise for an hour, the loaf doubles in size.

This way of thinking shows up all over our current education systems. The ingredients (students, teachers, curricula, number of hours in school, time on task) and the process have been "successful" millions of times before. Each step in the process is controllable, outcomes are predictable, and progress is easily assessed. Weekly spelling tests. End-of-unit quizzes. Midterm and final exams. This all seems so normal.

It is.

It's status quo normal.

We assume this is the way learning is meant to be. This way of seeing education is one of the unstated assumptions of our prevailing worldview, but in the history of humanity, it's a relatively young idea that emerged alongside factories, clockworks, and combustion engine vehicles.

Because complicated systems are made up of close cause-and-effect relationships, their functions and the relationships between their parts can be easily analyzed. This reducibility makes fixing problems efficient. We can troubleshoot and fix reducible systems at their component level because we know which parts are responsible for each function. If a car won't start, it might be a bad battery or starter, or perhaps it is out of gas. There's no need to kick the tires or test the brakes. Just collect data on the parts responsible for the problem (check the fuel gauge and battery charge), isolate the dysfunction, then fix or replace what's broken. Once fixed, a complicated system is put back together, ready to work again.

Complicated troubleshooting is how we make decisions in education as we know it. When we don't see an eight-year-old reading after months of school, we conclude something needs fixing. Maybe the child has dyslexia or perhaps the teacher isn't doing a good job. Both or either might be true, but in reality, neither are a sufficient complex explanation. Lots of children with dyslexia or ill-equipped teachers learn to read. In a complicated way of thinking, reading is not a whole complex behavior that cannot be adequately dissected into parts. Rather, reading is seen as the expected result of a recipe. You put in the right ingredients and the right amount of time, and you should get a child who reads.

We have all unwittingly tried to apply complicated troubleshooting to complex problems, but when things don't improve, or only improve for a while, we usually don't recognize that our approach is the problem. This is why education reforms don't work. Education reforms are complicated fix-it approaches that work in isolated cases and then usually only for a short time, often producing unwanted, unanticipated consequences. Fix-it solutions don't work because the root problem with schools today is their tenacious fixation on complicated, reductionist, machine-based thinking.

Why Does Western Society Love Complication?

Efficiency. Capitalism demands efficiency and complication delivers, at least in the short term. The goal of machines and factories, assembly lines, and standardized curriculum is maximum efficiency. Merriam-Webster defines *efficient* as "capable of producing desired results with little or no waste (as of time or materials)." The goal is to use as few resources as possible to produce a product, because fewer resources equal bigger profits. Waste is anything that doesn't contribute to the product. Waste is costly and inefficient. For this reason, activities that foster children's humanity have no place in industrial schools.

Play doesn't increase children's ability to sound out words? *Waste*.

No proven link between music education and increased test scores? *Waste*.

In early education, there are many well-known and not-so-well-known advocates for play-based learning. I've listened and read their heartfelt pleas for allowing ample time in children's day for play. I agree with all of it. The trouble is, as long as we run our schools on complication, play in school is like Aisha's elephant in the zoo. It is something that will be ignored or assimilated because it just doesn't fit the paradigm. Play introduces way too much complexity into the complicated way we currently do school, and all that beautiful, rich, complexity is seen through the machine paradigm as waste.

The intent of assembly lines, interstate highways, subway turnstiles, prepackaged school curricula, and any mechanism is to rein in, reduce, or eliminate complexity's wastefulness. Ironically, as we'll see later on, trying to control complexity by mechanistic efficiency is what produces waste. Complex, regenerative ways of living and learning eliminate waste via reciprocal relationships, but I'm getting ahead of myself.

We often associate efficiency with simplicity, but mechanistic systems do not increase efficiency by making things *simple*. They increase efficiency by controlling complexity with complicated rules. The tighter a complicated system tries to control or reduce complexity, the more complicated rules it creates and the more resources it takes to enforce those rules (which, ironically, is incredibly inefficient).

A second-grade Arizona teacher once showed me a clipboard

with pages of her daily schedule broken down into ten-minute segments. She was required to align her day with the district's scripted curriculum (a curriculum that tells teachers exactly what they are supposed to say and do as they teach a lesson) and pacing calendars. The school district required teachers to hang their schedule on clipboards in their classroom doorways so building principals could patrol the halls, checking clipboards and peeking in on classes, making sure teachers were "on pace" at any given moment, delivering the curriculum exactly as the district required. The daily schedules, scripted curriculum, and pacing calendars were all attempts to squeeze the normal human complexity of an elementary classroom into a very complicated way of doing school.

Complication and Learning

The trouble with complication in schools is that authentic learning is an extraordinarily complex process that generates something beyond the sum of the parts. The saying "systems are more than the sum of their parts" does *not* apply to complicated systems. Complicated systems are *intentionally* the sum of their parts, designed to not generate anything other than what the parts produce. Generating something beyond the sum of the parts would mean the system didn't adequately control complexity; therefore, it's inefficient. That's a problem for schools, because all real learning is more than the sum of the parts. When Aisha has her Aha! about animals, an entirely new conceptual understanding will emerge. It will be an understanding that goes beyond merely knowing that elephants and dogs are animals. It will include nuances about differences and questions about how relationships between animals work. True human learning requires frequent experiences with all kinds of complex phenomena. Phenomena that we experience with our hands, with how our body moves in space, with how they feel on our skin, or smell, or taste.

Despite this fundamental need for immersive complex experiences, our current education systems run on complication.

Standardized curriculum and national teaching competencies? *Complicated*.

Standardizing the number of hours in a school day and days in a year? *Complicated*.

Requiring those who teach toddlers to have a college degree? *Complicated*.

Age-segregated classrooms and "grade level" standards? *Complicated*.

In education as we know it, for the sake of efficiency (and purportedly in the name of fairness or equity), all students "learn" the same thing, in the same way, at the same pace. All second graders in the class I described above "learn" the same spelling words, use the same spelling worksheets, and take the same spelling test at the same time on the same day each week. One or two students may have a different, individual plan because they are in "special" education, but they are not the norm. They are, in this system, intentionally and explicitly, outside the norm.

In the name of efficiency, schools, as we know them, use complicated methods that disrupt and attempt to control the complexity of authentic human learning. Regenerative learning is about reviving authentically complex ways of knowing and learning that the complicated industrial era mindset has destroyed.

Because authentic learning is highly complex, complicated approaches turn what happens in schools into something that isn't real learning at all. During an era when we only needed people to throw factory switches and follow directions, these systems were far more fit for function (though not fit for people). That era is long gone. Our educational systems are hamstrung in their inherent complicated structure, and most people crafting education policy have no idea how to do anything other than create more complication. When they run into a complicated dead end, they swirl. Many (most?) have never even considered there might be other ways. Complication is, after all, how they (and we) were taught to think.

Our global problems emerged from our current ways of thinking. Our current ways of thinking cannot fix them.

Knowing the Drill

Several years ago, I took a temporary end-of-year position with San Diego Unified, the school district I attended growing up. In my temporary job, I served Walt Whitman Elementary, located about five miles from James Whitcomb Riley Elementary, where I went to grade school. Even though it was my first time working as a psychologist in California, I knew exactly what to expect my first morning on the job. The office would be well-marked and easy to find, with itinerant staff sign-in sheets held in a binder or clipboard on the counter with a pen tied to it for safekeeping. The principal's and nurse's offices would be near or in the front office. Classrooms and playgrounds for lower grades would be grouped together and separated from the upper grades. Adult bathrooms would be separate from bathrooms for children.

I knew The Drill.

I had been hired near the end of the school year to clear out a backlog of special education evaluations. To do my job, I needed easy access to student records, which meant I must quickly build rapport with the office manager and principal (in that order). It mattered little that my credentials were emblazoned on my ID badge; rapport was more important than qualifications. They would decide where I worked and if I had an adult-sized chair and desk.

On my first morning, after exchanging pleasantries, the office manager gave me a key to a small office in the next building. I stepped outside and caught a whiff of jasmine. Suddenly, rather than being a forty-something professional at Whitman Elementary, I was nine years old following my fourth-grade friends back to class after a Riley Elementary recess.

It was the strongest déjà vu I've ever felt.

I blinked hard. What triggered such a vivid recollection? Was it just the scent of a San Diego springtime? Looking around, I saw

Whitman's long low buildings with windows like a checkerboard and solid doors spaced every forty feet or so. The paint was different (thankfully), but the buildings were not merely similar to the school of my childhood, Whitman was an exact copy of Riley. I shook off the reverie and stepped onto the walkway. I found myself trailing a line of children. Just like my fourth-grade self, they also knew The Drill.

The Drill Is Caught, Not Taught

Why have schools changed so little in the decades since I walked the halls of Riley Elementary? The phone in my pocket is nothing like the phone in my childhood home. I can't remember the last time I spoke face to face with a bank teller. I do all my banking online. Why, with all the dramatic innovations in our world, have schools remained untouched for forty years?

Because they do so well what they were initially intended to do.

Mass public education grew up alongside industrialization because industrial capitalism needed it. Industrialization needed the general populace to think in ways that made them good line workers. Manufacturers needed workers to be dependent on others for their living, willingly compliant with the working conditions decided by someone else who held more power. Employers needed human cogs in an industrial machine that hadn't yet figured out how to automatize the functions people performed.

The primary purpose of schools was to create enough people who knew (and followed) The Drill—the *how* to think. Schools are often criticized for only teaching kids *what* to think, not *how* to think. That's a dangerous misconception.

Schools use *what* to think to teach *how* to think.

Not the other way around.

Training people *how* to think is the primary purpose of schools. The *how* to think is baked into the complicated structure of each school day. In Chapter 2, I touched on the role mental models play in translating paradigmatic assumptions into daily life. Nowhere is this truer than in schools. The Drill is a collection of mental models that school children encounter day after day after day for years. Two of the most powerful types of mental models—scripts and scenes—significantly influence how we think because they organize our lives into stories, and stories are perhaps the most powerful way humans learn and form memories. They are the nonconscious way we learn *how* to think so we can function as expected in our society.

Scripts are action sequences. Scenes are the ways people and things are present in a space where scripts happen. Scripts and scenes are so embedded in daily life we learn to act automatically in alignment with them without needing to be explicitly taught. When I walk into a fast-food restaurant, I decide what to eat while waiting in line. I order at the counter when it's my turn, pay, wait for my order, then eat. The scene and the script are entirely different at a fine dining restaurant. Fancy restaurants don't have a counter with teenage cashiers sporting paper hats.

Scenes convey important information about what script people should use in all sorts of situations. When you walk into a meeting room with chairs positioned around small tables covered in large newsprint and scattered with markers, you know people will behave much differently than if you walk in a room set with chairs in rows facing a podium. No one needs to "teach" you how to behave in each of these situations. The way the environment is set up prompts you to act in certain ways.

Separating, Sorting, and Sequencing

Schools immerse children every day in a set of specialized scripts and scenes that nonconsciously communicate the patterns and mental models of the prevailing machine paradigm. These scripts and scenes are repeated day after day, year after year, seeping deeply into the nonconscious depths of young minds and profoundly influencing how they think and act. Three mental models, in particular separating, sorting, and sequencing, do a powerful job teaching how to think in ways aligned with the machine paradigm without a penny spent on curriculum.

Schools begin separating even before children set foot in kindergarten. Each spring and over the summer, school districts "round up" preschool children so school personnel can assess them and separate those who are "ready" for school from those who are not. During kindergarten roundup, parents and children go to different areas to see how they, both children and adults, will react to being separated.

Starting school, separation continues. For many children, preschool or kindergarten is the first time they are separated from their families and home on a daily basis. Children are separated in school from their siblings and often from neighbors and extended family members. Other than one year of middle school choir, my twins were never in the same public-school class.

The scripts and scenes of separation (saying goodbye to young children when dropping them off at school) are an unquestioned "just the way things are" assumption that has emerged from industrialized capitalism. For parents to fill the workforce pipeline, they've got to separate from their children; the younger the better. Rarely does anyone question if separating young children from family members is beneficial or even necessary. The prevailing paradigm's mental models of separation have so saturated our society that daily separation at age five (or younger) is assumed to be a normal part of growing up. Yet for millennia humans have lived and learned in extended families, spending their days with those they are related to.

In school, children are not only separated from family, they're also separated from adults in curious ways. For example, at home or in public, say at a restaurant or a park, do children use a different bathroom than adults? Eat separately from adults? Not typically, but in school they do. Separating children from adults is a key mental model of the prevailing paradigm.

Kids go to school.

Parents go to work.

Separation keeps the system going.

Sorting is a special case of separation. People are sorted in all sorts of ways in schools. Children are sorted into grade levels according to age and, within classes, by (supposed) ability. Children are sorted by a binary concept of gender (boys' line, girls' line), which poses tremendous challenges for children who fit neither category and for the educators trying to accommodate their identities. Children are also sorted by the languages they speak. The long-term effect of redlining real-estate practices means schools are often places where children are sorted by race and family or neighborhood wealth.

People in schools are sorted by who stewards knowledge and who does not. Educators hold and dispense knowledge. Children receive it. Nonprofessionals clean, manage, cook, and drive, but they are not stewards of knowledge. Children learn these distinctions early on. Once I was testing a six-year-old for a district's "gifted" program. Early in the test, I posed a practice question that asked how two things were similar. The child looked at me quizzically and asked, "Don't you know? Why are you asking me? I'm a kid. You're supposed to tell me."

People are not the only things sorted in schools. Knowledge and (in the early years, especially) development are sorted too. Knowledge is sorted into math, reading, and (if a school is well-resourced) science and maybe music. Development is sorted into cognitive, language, social-emotional, and physical. When I encounter the slicing and dicing of development, I always find my forehead planted in my palm. Human development simply does not work that way. Just as there is no aspect of development that isn't physical, there is no aspect of development that isn't cognitive. There isn't a single emotion that is not physiologically induced or that has no physiological consequence. There isn't a single emotion that the brain does not regulate or respond to.

Even so, every single US state has a set of early learning "standards" that sort development into these contrived "domains."

Sorting knowledge in discreet categories allows it to be easily sequenced into years, with a curriculum year sequenced from a starting to an ending point. Curriculum is traditionally defined as scope (the content to be taught) and sequence (the order in which it is taught). Curriculum is further separated, sorted, and sequenced into weekly or monthly themes or topics. Teachers regularly follow "pacing" calendars or schedules to make sure they align the sorted curriculum into the appropriately sorted timeframes. To "learn" the sorted and sequenced information, grades are sequenced from lower to upper, with children promoting year by year as they "move through the curriculum."

Equally profound and, given what we know about human learning, even more baffling, *time* is sorted into learning and nonlearning segments such as recess, passing periods, and lunch. Sorting time allows governments to hold schools accountable for "instructional" time.

This is simply not the way human learning works.

I can't emphasize this enough. There is nothing in anecdotal or scientific evidence that even hints that this is the way humans actually learn.

Nothing.

Pause for a moment and consider that everything children and youth need to learn during their growing up years can be accomplished without *any* of the separating, sorting, or sequencing that occurs every day in schools as we know them. We could argue that these operations are designed for crowd control or for fairness. But the truth is, not only are these operational mechanisms not needed for humans to learn, they are counterproductive.

What in the world is going on? If we don't need to separate and sort people or knowledge or time, or sequence curriculum for people to learn, what is the purpose of these mechanisms and all the scripts and scenes that support them?

Rules of the Drill

By immersing young humans in separating, sorting, and sequencing scripts and scenes, children quickly learn *how* to align their thinking with the machine paradigm. I call these machine-paradigm ways of thinking the Rules of the Drill. They are the means by which schools perpetuate the prevailing machine worldview and by which individuals learn how to perform for the profit of others in a capitalist-industrialized society. Following these rules might allow the majority of people to make money, but in the process, they rob humans of agency, voice, creativity, and joy.

Rule of the Drill #1: Think passively. Children learn quickly that someone else does their thinking for them. When kindergarteners line up for recess, they learn that someone else chooses when, where, and for how long people take a break. They learn that people in authority make those decisions for others, and in order for "others" to be considered "good" they cooperate with authority cheerfully.

In my first semester of doctoral studies, a professor told the story about a learning scientist who interviewed kindergarten children at the start of the school year. Among other questions, the researcher asked, "When do you go to the bathroom?" One by one the children looked at her with furrowed brows and replied with some version of, "When I need to." She came back at the end of the first semester and asked the same question. This time the children said, "When my teacher tells me to."

Rule of the Drill #2: Think in parts. Kids quickly learn each "subject" has its own set of scripts and scenes. Reading and math use different materials and tools. Reading has colorful books with lots of words and maybe plastic letters or sentence strips. Math has worksheets with numbers and maybe blocks. Art usually takes place in a separate room, not in the room where "real" learning happens. Sometimes subjects overlap or have similarities, but primarily each subject not only happens at its own time and in its own way, but subjects are also not related to each other. Math has nothing to do with reading and vice versa. Seventh grade English is separate from and taught with different texts and usually by different faculty than eighth grade English. English is separate from chemistry. Chemistry is taught in a different wing and takes place in a separate scene called a lab. There are completely different scripts for how students engage in a chemistry class versus an English class. Classes are distinct, unrelated parts of a high school education. I read Thomas Kuhn's *Structure of Scientific Revolutions* as a high school senior. I was surprised by the idea that someone could be both a science historian and a philosopher. I had no idea science, history, and philosophy had anything to do with each other.

Rule of the Drill #3: Think linearly. From day one, children learn to think in lines. Placing their bodies in a line and walking at a common pace with their classmates is an essential early grades skill. Students line up outside classrooms. And for recess. They line up for lunch. And again if they ride a bus. In most schools, classrooms are also in a line, down a long corridor. Until recently, even in the early grades, classroom desks were arranged in lines.

The curriculum is also linear. One starts at the beginning and works through it, from beginning to end. A "good" curriculum circles back to previous content, allowing ideas to be presented repeatedly, but the direction of the curriculum is a line, from one point to another, like going up a staircase. Topics (supposedly) build on one another. Reconfiguring ideas, which might require discarding something learned earlier, has no place in this linear model. Grade levels are also linear. Children start at kindergarten and go from first through twelfth grade. It is an anomaly if a grade is repeated or skipped. Completing all grades adds up to a diploma. A diploma is the sum of its parts.

Rule of the Drill #4: Think dichotomously. Dichotomy is either/or, black-and-white, red versus blue thinking. It is the lowest level of concept formation. Very young children begin to understand their world by distinguishing mommy from not-the-mommy. Throughout much of the first few years of life, this rudimentary way of thinking is important. Young children learn some things are okay to do (play with my toys) others are not okay (play with knives). Some animals are dogs, some, like elephants, are not.

At the heart of cognitive maturity is the capacity to think in nuanced, nondichotomous ways, and yet schools immerse children in dichotomy all the way through high school commencement. Answers are either right or wrong. You either complete an assignment or not. You are either a learner or a teacher. You are either the valedictorian or not. You either graduate or not. For all of us who were educated in this model, it's nearly impossible to imagine an educational system where "assignments" are an anomaly, and if they do exist, students decide when they are "complete." How could you grade that?

Such rigorous practice in dichotomy leaves little time for learning the nuances of complex thinking, to consider multiple points of view, or to understand there are often multiple "right" ways to approach a situation. Dichotomous thinking sets people up for asserting and defending their opinions and rejecting all shades of gray. Dichotomous thinking is, perhaps, the greatest obstacle to complexity thinking because complexity lives in shades of gray. It is also the greatest hindrance to empathizing with those with whom we disagree. The commonalities between diverse perspectives also live in shades of gray.

Rule of the Drill #5: Think competitively. One of the most powerful ways that separating, sorting, and sequencing influences children is by fostering competition. From kindergarten attendance awards to senior class rankings, schools preach collaboration while rewarding competition. In my second year as a school psychologist, a thirty-year veteran kindergarten teacher asked for help with one of her students. We met briefly to discuss her concerns and arrange a time for me to observe the child. When I arrived at the classroom for the observation, the teacher was seated at her desk with children lined up in front of a long bank of windows. Each child held a piece of paper with a crayoned picture drawn on one side. The children's morning task was to replicate the teacher's drawing, then bring their product to her for her to grade. As fate would have it, the child in question stepped up to her desk just as I walked in the door.

She waved me over. "Perfect timing! See what I'm talking about?" She held up the boy's picture, then pointed to her drawing. "That's what it is supposed to look like! He can't even copy a simple drawing."

When I recall this incident, some thirty years later, and wonder what became of that child, I also think of what the other children learned that day. From the first week of the first year of school, children learn to compare themselves to other children and determine how they measure up. They quickly learn that being best *is* best. They are measured and judged, so they measure and judge. They learn to compete for resources, status, and sometimes their very dignity. If they learn, as the children in this class did, that humiliation lurks in the shadows, they will vie for status, hoping to create for themselves at least a smidgeon of safety.

Paradigms Have Consequences

I doubt the kindergarten teacher in the story above intended to obliterate that child's self-respect, but when people live day-in and day-out in schools that operate by the Rules of the Drill, emotional safety is rarely a consideration.

Separating, sorting, and sequencing mental models infiltrate and influence our grownup lives as well. In her book *Soil Science for Regenerative Agriculture*, permaculture design specialist Amélie des Plantes comments on how this complicated way of thinking has led to a frightening depletion of fertile soil around the globe: "Today's scientists know little about the biochemical activity that goes on in the soil. Segregating our knowledge about soil into Soil Biology, Soil Bio physics, Agronomy, and

Soil Chemistry has hindered our view of the big picture of what soil is."

Stripping humans of our capacity to see wholes and think in complexity has led to disastrous consequences. I told the story of Castle Bravo to open this chapter not only to emphasize how long we've needed to change our ways of thinking, but to highlight how separating, sorting, and sequencing mindsets cause catastrophes. The nuclear physicists who designed Castle Bravo did not *intend* their creation to be a 15-megaton behemoth. But they used complicated thinking that obscured the complexity of the situation. Only 40 percent of the lithium in Bravo's payload was supposed to ignite while the other 60 percent, a different type of lithium, was to serve as ballast and remain inert. The explosion was projected to destroy Bikini Atoll and the surrounding sea, not inhabited villages on other atolls. The "safe zone" was determined from these intentions and the understanding that Castle Bravo would be tested when trade winds blew away from inhabited Marshallese atolls.

In the scientists' lab, under exponentially less complex test conditions, the bomb worked as designed. The two types of lithium behaved separately. Something very different happened in real-world complexity. The unprecedented speed and size of Castle Bravo's initial explosion caused *all* the lithium to ignite, creating a blast nearly three times larger than anticipated.

The scientists brought their best complicated thinking to designing the bomb. The smartest nuclear physicists on the planet assumed they could control its deadly force by manipulating its components. They failed to consider that the bomb might generate something beyond the sum of its parts when unleashed in the complex reality of the Western Pacific.

Similarly, complicated thinking allowed military commanders and US politicians to give the go-ahead to blow up an irreplaceable oceanic atoll and all the life on and around it to test weapons that could annihilate humanity.

Our global problems emerged from our current ways of thinking. Our current ways of thinking cannot fix them.

Our individual and collective failure to see and think in complexity, and instead to follow the Rules of the Drill, remains the single greatest threat to our existence as a species. Education as we know it replicates the industrial era's mechanistic way of thinking that is destroying Earth, day after day, year after year, child after child. This book is intended to empower you to regenerate your capacity to clearly see our complex world and embrace your place in the self-organizing groups of people who are committed to creating just and sustainable societies. It is intended to help you make choices for yourself, your community, and your world that will help our society raise children who are native complexity thinkers: children for whom seeing and thinking in complexity is just the way the world works.

4

START WITH SCHOOLS

An industrial economy is a linear economy.
We take from Nature, use it and then throw it away
with the consequence that it ends up in landfills,
in rivers and oceans and in the atmosphere. We need
to replace this linear economy with a cyclical economy.
~ SATISH KUMAR

The artifacts of education are diplomas, but the sensemaking
is much, much, much deeper. Even the smell of a milk carton
can bring the loneliness of third grade.
~ NORA BATESON

Ron, then dean of the University of Arizona's College of Education, looked at me, shrugged, and tilted his head toward the speaker phone on his desk, indicating I should respond to the caller on the line. The woman on the phone, Karen, was the chief program officer at a relatively new state agency, Arizona's Early Childhood Development and Health Board. We were talking with Karen about how our college might convene a team of faculty researchers across Arizona's three public universities to evaluate First Things First, the public-facing name for the early childhood programs funded by her agency. The evaluation budget was $27 million. It would be the largest contract our college had ever landed. I was a doctoral candidate in Ron's department, and he had hired me to manage proposal development and help design the study.

Our phone call with Karen started with the usual pleasantries. Then Ron asked Karen the holy grail of evaluation questions: "What do you want to learn that you don't already know?"

"Does it work?"

That's when Ron shrugged.

Of course, this was what Karen (and her entire agency) wanted to know. Arizona taxpayers had invested hundreds of millions of dollars in this effort. The organization's leadership needed evidence to justify creating a new government agency, especially in what was then a deeply conservative state.

But there was a problem. Karen asked a question no evaluation could directly answer. Karen wanted to know if "it" (the system as a whole) worked. In other words, she wanted to use *complicated* approaches (evaluation methods that answer cause-and-effect questions) to determine a *complicated* outcome (does it work or not) to evaluate a highly *complex* system. How could we still win the contract if we told her that the learning sciences—heck, any of the sciences—were ill-equipped to answer questions about the outcomes of an entire complex social system? If I were to be frank, I would tell Karen we could evaluate parts of the system (because that is what complicated evaluations do), but even the most sophisticated methodology cannot validly evaluate whether a complex social system "works." Not wanting her to hang up and hire an evaluation firm that would be less candid, I posed a question of my own.

"Karen, what is the 'it' you want to evaluate, and what do you mean by 'work'?" As we awaited Karen's response, my mind wandered to the work of Dr. Edward Lorenz, a meteorologist and mathematician at Massachusetts Institute of Technology.

When a WTF Moment Starts a New Science

You may have noticed that I move between talking about schools and talking about society and the paradigm that guides them both. You may have wondered why we shouldn't all just go after the machine paradigm and shut that sucker down. If you're so inclined, have at it. But if we are to invest our efforts so that we have the best chance at long-lasting influence, influence that has the best chance of preserving our planet and species and setting conditions for all on Earth to flourish, well, we've got to start with schools. This chapter is about why that's true.

If you've ever heard of the "butterfly effect," you're familiar with the work of meteorological scientist Dr. Edward Lorenz. At the 1972 annual meeting of the American Association for the Advancement of Science, Dr. Lorenz famously asked, "Does the flap of a butterfly's wings in Brazil set off a tornado in Texas?" Spoiler, his answer was no, although small differences in complex systems matter quite a bit.

Lorenz's fascination with his famous question started ten years earlier in his MIT lab when he made a miniscule mistake that changed his career and launched a new science. Dr. Lorenz had printed out a weather graph but decided to restart the printout so he could include additional data. He located the point on the graph where he wanted to begin reprinting and read *from the graph he had printed out* the number that represented the starting data point. He entered that number into the computer. His 1960s printer was insufferably slow, so while it chugged along, outputting the new graph, Ed went down the hall for a cup of coffee. When he came back, he noticed something odd. The graph he had just printed deviated significantly from the first printout, even though both were printed from the same computer model and dataset.

This was Lorenz's WTF moment.

A big sloppy Huh?

A moment that would forever alter his life's work, and for us inform our understanding of why schools are absolutely necessary for societal change.

It didn't take Dr. Lorenz long to figure out what had happened. His computer stored data to six digits after the decimal point. The starting data point he selected for the second printout was .506127. But the first printout only showed three digits past the decimal point, reading .506. That is the number he entered to start the second print run.

The data point he entered for the second run was off by .000127, but somehow that tiny error made a big unexpected difference in the trajectory of the weather prediction. As Dr. James Gleick in his book *Chaos: Making a New Science* explains, "He decided to look more closely at the way two nearly identical runs of weather flowed apart. He copied one of the wavy lines of output onto a transparency and laid it over the other. The first two humps matched detail for detail. Then one line began to lag a hairsbreadth behind. By the time the two runs reached the next hump, they were distinctly out of phase. By the third and fourth hump, all similarity had vanished."

Prior to Lorenz's error, his assumptions were shaped by the paradigm he had adopted as a classically trained, linear-thinking scientist: differences at one point in prediction lead to similarly sized differences at another point. Predictability is the heart of linear thinking. It assumes that small variances in data can (and should) be ignored because they are inconsequential to predictions of cause and effect. This is why statistical analyses disregard small errors. We commonly think statistics are precise, but they're merely estimation and probability. If you can accurately predict 95 percent of the time, you're good. There's even a technical term for how much error a scientist is willing to allow; it's called a *p* value. Researchers usually set it at .05, although sometimes it is set at .01. Somehow, the researcher is supposed to know in advance how much room to allow for error.

Lorenz could have circular-filed the printouts, assuming his Huh? moment was just a computer glitch. He could have stuck with the assumption that error is nothing more than ignorable random fluctuations. He could have, like our toddler friend Aisha, called his elephant a doggy and ignored it because it didn't fit his existing mental model.

But he didn't.

Lorenz stayed buckled up with the uncomfortable implications of his mistake: that there are some circumstances where small differences early on lead to much greater differences down the road. This is precisely why the only path forward out of industrialism and into a regenerative, restorative future lies with schools. Lorenz's willingness to stay with this paradigm-challenging inquiry contributed to the birth of chaos theory and the science of nonlinear systems. That science gives us perhaps the most compelling reason for focusing our society-shifting efforts on schools: the initial conditions in which complex systems (like, you know, humans) emerge are disproportionately and overwhelmingly important to long-term outcomes.

Nonlinearity and Change

To help us wrap our minds around disproportional change and what it has to do with paradigm shifts and schools, let's first consider what we're accustomed to: linear, proportional change. Linear cause-and-effect relationships are like a staircase. When you walk upstairs, each step moves you both vertically and horizontally. Think of the vertical dimension as one variable and the horizontal as the other. When you go up, you also go forward. When you go forward, you also go up. They are inextricably related to each other.

Within limits, stairs can have a variety of rise heights and run lengths, but building codes require the rise and run to remain the same for the entire staircase. It's a safety thing. When you're walking up or down stairs you get into a rhythm, and if the height or depth changes, you're likely to fall. The proportions between rise and run must be the same from bottom to top.

We like the predictability that comes with linearity. But when it comes to affecting big, paradigmatic change, linearity is a problem. If you want large-scale change, you don't want to set linear conditions. You don't want predictable, proportional change. You want disproportional change.

Our global problems emerged from our *linear* ways of thinking.

Our *linear* ways of thinking cannot fix them.

We need to know how to influence nonlinearity and disproportionality.

But.

Disproportional change scares the hell out of us.

Nonlinearity is unpredictable. One day you're flying home when you catch a CNN report on an airport TV about a virus across the Pacific, and seven days later that virus is a full-blown pandemic. One day your house is worth $100,000 more than you paid for it five years before, so you disregard news about some weird type of mortgages that have nothing to do with you. Two months later, you go to ReFi and find out your home's value has plummeted to $200,000 less than what you owe. Ouch. So much for a little wiggle room in your monthly budget.

Nonlinearity and Schools

As much as we don't like the unpredictable nature of nonlinear dynamics, this complex phenomenon has a special case that is particularly relevant to why schools matter: small differences *early* in the development of a complex system have a disproportionately large and lasting impact on the system's nature and trajectory. Further, as I'll discuss in the next chapter, complex systems custom fit themselves to the conditions in which they emerge. Put these two dynamics together and it means that complex systems are highly sensitive to initial conditions.

Of the instances in which initial conditions have disproportional influence on complex systems, human development tops the list. A whole new way of doing school is critical to creating a regenerative future because schools shape the lives of humans during their most susceptible developmental phase in ways that affect their entire life trajectory and the society in which they live.

Arizona, along with many US states and countries around the

world, has invested heavily in early education because research consistently shows that what children experience in their early years affects their performance in school and adulthood. Entire volumes have been written on the benefits of high-quality early learning, but for our purposes here, the critical point is that what happens early in human development is exponentially more consequential to long-term outcomes than what happens later in life.

From what conditions do we want young humans to emerge? What do we want to have influence in their lives? If we want to perpetuate the machine paradigm, separating, sorting, and sequencing experiences are our best bet. Those conditions have produced industrial-era workforces for decades. But if we want generations of people who are adept at interfacing with complexity and for whom living in communities where everyone thrives is just the way things are, then we need to start by creating regenerative schools.

Does It Work?

My cubicle was shiny, new, and entirely empty, save for a thick document resting in the center of my desk with a sticky note stuck on the cover. It was my first day working for First Things First, Arizona's Early Childhood Development and Health Board, almost three years to the day after the conversation Ron and I had with Karen, who remained the agency's chief program officer and would soon become my supervisor. I was a top candidate for a senior director position but was offered a director position in the evaluation department because, I was told, there was an immediate need for my expertise. Would I be willing to serve in that capacity while the hiring process for the senior role wrapped up? I had agreed.

I plopped my workbag on the desk and picked up the document. It was a draft of the kindergarten readiness evaluation that the multi-university evaluation consortium had conducted.

I had helped design the evaluation. The sticky note, from the senior director of evaluation, my new interim boss, read, "This is the third draft of the kindergarten readiness evaluation report. The first two were unacceptable. Your thoughts?"

I didn't need to read the report to know what some of the problems were. I had spent the two years between helping to land the evaluation contract for the University of Arizona and my first day as an employee of First Things First as a tenure-track professor at Arizona State University. A colleague of mine at ASU had taken the lead on the kindergarten readiness evaluation. We worked on the same campus and in the same department, so we saw each other often.

The kindergarten readiness evaluation was intentionally designed to work well with the complexity of evaluating the development of children who were age-eligible for kindergarten. The design team had selected assessment protocols that had been developed by the US federal government for the Kindergarten Readiness Longitudinal Study, a massive study of over 26,000 preschoolers. The assessment protocols were abbreviated versions of commonly used developmental tests, which allowed researchers to collect reliable data on large numbers of children without needing multiple lengthy sessions with kids and families. Unfortunately, the implementation team disregarded that decision and instead used full versions of several very complicated assessment tools. To be properly trained in the full versions would have required graduate coursework and several hours of supervised practice. The data collectors had received neither.

I sat down to read the report. The executive summary claimed that overall, children entering kindergarten in Arizona had solid preacademic skills. I put the report down and closed my eyes. First Things First existed because voters in a ruby red US state had overwhelmingly passed an initiative to tax themselves. Tax initiatives to fund programming for young children rarely pass, but this one did because Arizonans could clearly see that many young children were not "ready" for kindergarten. I finished reading the report and wrote my critique.

A few months later, as a senior director with the agency, I sat in a small office across the street from the University of Arizona's College of Education with another colleague. She and I had both earned our educational psychology doctorates across the street three years earlier. The last time I had seen her we were backstage, straightening each other's mortarboards and giddily snapping pictures before our hooding ceremony. Now I was auditing her work, knowing that she had not been the one to make the decisions that led to the debacle we faced, and knowing that she, through no fault of her own, would likely lose her job because the evaluation project was likely to be shuttered for nonperformance. For a few moments, we sat in silence. Then I started asking questions.

The most pressing issue was the fact that the evaluation was to include a "representative sample" of children from across the state. At the time, well over 40 percent of Arizona's incoming kindergarteners were from Spanish-speaking homes. That meant that at least 40 percent of the children in the study should also be from Spanish-speaking homes. Instead, such children represented less than 10 percent of study participants. Why were Spanish-speaking children so underrepresented?

Several obstacles hindered efforts to obtain a representative sample of children, but the biggest problem had to do with data collection snafus. The Spanish-speaking evaluators were unclear about discontinue rules. Nearly all standardized, individually administered developmental tests require administrating items until the child has made a predetermined number of errors. Each test has different discontinue rules. It could be three in a row wrong, or maybe three out of five. In any case, the Spanish-speaking evaluators had not applied the rules consistently, yielding inaccurate results.

When the assessment forms were reviewed and the mistake caught, the evaluation team retrained the evaluators so they could readminister the tests. Unfortunately, most kids or their families didn't want to take the tests again. Even if data collectors could reengage the children, the new results would be tainted by "practice effects." You know how you get better after you've taken a test a few times? Those are practice effects. When you're taking a driver's license test, everyone hopes you get better every time you take the test. But in a research study, practice effects spoil results.

Ultimately, the evaluation team scrapped all but the few cases of children from Spanish-speaking households whose assessments had been properly administered. That meant the overall results did not reflect the actual population of children entering kindergarten in Arizona, defeating the purpose of the study.

What does this have to do with changing society by starting with schools? I've told you just one of dozens of stories I could tell about how even the most well-meaning and educated people working to improve our education systems make both inconsequential and major mistakes because they are conceptually hogtied by complicated thinking. We've all been trained to think the same way Dr. Edward Lorenz had been trained to think: that small changes don't change research outcomes enough to worry about. My colleagues did not think it would affect the outcome of the evaluation if they switched from abbreviated research protocols to full-blown assessments. But it did. The evaluation team decided it really didn't matter if they based their conclusions on a smaller sample of Spanish-speaking children. But it did.

When the professionals who make decisions about education systems remain entrenched in the mechanistic, linear ways of thinking they were taught in school, we end up with educational systems that perpetuate mechanistic ways of thinking.

Karen never did tell us what she meant by "Does it work?" I wish she had. If she had said that she wanted to know if the agency's programs would better prepare children to succeed in the workforce pipeline, I imagine I would have said, "With twenty-seven million dollars we can probably figure that out."

But if she had said that she wanted to know if the statewide programs would prepare children to be loving stewards of a precious planet, to assume their responsibility to set conditions conducive to life, and to prioritize mutual thriving for everyone, I would have had to say, "No. That's not what education as we know it is intended to do, and we don't need to spend twenty-seven million dollars to figure that out."

5

Regenerative Life and Learning

The education of the future is faced with a universal problem because our compartmentalized, piecemeal, disjointed learning is deeply drastically inadequate to grasp realities and problems which are ever more global, transnational, multidimensional, transversal, polydisciplinary and planetary.

~ Dr. Edgar Morin

Complicated thinking is rooted in the work of French philosopher and mathematician René Descartes, the founder of analytical geometry. Descartes famously said, "I think, therefore I am." His work has had profound and lasting impact on how we think, and therefore are. Dr. Peter Checkland, professor emeritus of systems thinking at Lancaster University, writes, "René Descartes taught Western civilization that the thing to do with complexity was to break it up into component parts and tackle them separately. *The lesson has been well learned, and the idea is deeply embodied...in anyone who has a Western-style education....* The Cartesian legacy provides us with an unnoticed framework—a set of intellectual pigeon-holes—into which we place new knowledge we acquire" (emphasis is mine).

The unnoticed pigeon-holing of knowledge is core to mechanistic thinking. It means everyone raised in a Western society has been taught that slicing and dicing our complex humanity and compartmentalizing our infinitely complex world into bite-size concepts is just the way things are. Philosopher

Dr. Mary Midgley points to the heart of the problem, saying that this mechanistic way of thinking is "so 'automatic'—that people scarcely notice it, let alone criticize it or see it as dangerous."

She's talking about you and me.

We scarcely notice the slicing and dicing, let alone criticize it or see it as dangerous.

If we or our descendants are ever to find humanity thriving on a renewed and flourishing planet, we need schools that foster regenerative values and mindsets. Throughout the remainder of this book, I use the term *regenerative*, borrowed from biologist Dr. Daniel Wahl, business coach Dr. Carol Sanford, and educator Satish Kumar, to refer to a complex worldview that I and many others see as a potential life-honoring, emerging paradigm. At its core, a regenerative paradigm prioritizes mutual well-being for all. It sees everyone and everything as part of a connected whole. A regenerative paradigm shifts our perspective from seeing Earth as a resource for human consumption to seeing humans as privileged to live responsibly as intelligent participants in the web of life, and for regenerating, as much as possible, that which humans have already destroyed while adopting ways of living that set conditions conducive to life.

This isn't a burdensome, mandated responsibility. Rather, it is akin to the Hawaiian word *kuleana*. Loosely translated, kuleana means responsibility, but there is more to it than just having a job to do. It is a privileged responsibility. Something only entrusted to those who are prepared and willingly accept. It also holds the notion that the person with the kuleana and whatever or whomever they are responsible for have a *mutually beneficial, reciprocal relationship*. So, when humans accept the kuleana for setting conditions conducive to life, we do it with the understanding that we are in a reciprocal relationship with Earth and all the life Earth holds. All benefit when we hold this privilege in deep regard. Much of the remainder of this book is about what those conditions are, how we set them, and what is required to commit ourselves to this responsibility.

The first thing we need to do is to start thinking in a whole new way.

A Whole New Way

Regenerative learning invites us (and our children) to understand that we are, and we are surrounded by, complex phenomena that are *more than* and *other than* the sum of their parts. How is that possible? How can something be more than and other than the sum of its parts? And why is that possibility important?

It's important because the things that really matter, such as the planet and the creatures that live on it, and all natural phenomena, including humans, including our children, can only be adequately understood as whole phenomena. The machine paradigm has obscured our understanding of the uniqueness, beauty, and power of whole phenomena. If the slicing and dicing of human development and learning is at the core of what's wrong in our current education system and, I would argue, our economic, monetary, and political systems as well, then we've got to buckle up and learn to think in wholes.

Thinking in wholes helps us understand that complex systems are not only *more than* but also something *other than* the sum of their parts.

Children are *other than* the sum of their parts.

Learning is *other than* the sum of its parts.

Education systems are *other than* the sum of their parts.

Earth is *other than* the sum of its parts.

When something is *other than* the sum of its parts, we cannot adequately understand it by analyzing its pieces. If you're wondering how in the world we can understand complex phenomena if we can't analyze parts, Einstein had an answer. *Learn to think in a whole new way.*

Those three words, whole, new, and way, are more than cliché. The defining characteristic of complexity is that it generates new wholes that are something other than the sum of the parts. They are key to noticing and rejecting complicated pigeon-holing of things that cannot be properly understood when sliced and diced. If we are truly committed to educating future generations in ways that honor their humanity and prepares them to live in harmony with each other on a thriving planet, we need to do everything we can to shift from thinking in parts and pieces to thinking in wholes. This chapter gives you a solid understanding of *whole* and *new*. Part 2 is devoted to the *way*, the *how to* live, think, learn, and teach in complexity.

Wholeness

Humans are whole phenomena. Every cell in our bodies carries our unique DNA, yet you will not find the whole of who I am in any individual cell. I don't exist in my parts. You cannot find me in my spleen. My brain does not make me, me. My heart doesn't either. I am more than and other than both or either. You cannot add up my parts and find me. I cannot add up your parts and find you. The me that is me can only be found emerging from the relationships of the parts, not in the parts nor the sum of them. The same is true for you.

The idea of seeing and understanding things as whole might be hard to wrap our heads around, but this way of thinking has not only been around for as long as humans have walked the earth, we're also surrounded by it every day. Complexity thinking gives us ways of understanding patterns of wholeness and newness that complicated ways of thinking just can't.

Take bugs, for instance. If you find a locust-looking bug hanging out all by itself in your garden, I'll tell you right now, it probably isn't a locust. Locusts are a particular type of grasshopper, the type that can, under certain circumstance, *swarm*. These particular types of grasshoppers move in a pattern that allows them to feed off of bountifully growing vegetation during rainy seasons. In the next section, I'll share more about what scientists have discovered about how and why locusts swarm and what that has to do with influencing complex systems change. The important part to know now is that a *swarm* refers to the complex other-than-the-sum-of-the-parts phenomena that emerges when individuals collectively *self-organize* around a small set of *Simple Rules*.

Newness

If we want a whole new regenerative way of doing school to emerge, we need a whole slew of people who understand *Simple Rules*, *self-organizing*, and *emergence*. These ideas are inextricably connected, so it's best to describe them together. *Self-organizing* happens when individuals start following the same set of *Simple Rules*. Simple Rules are not merely rules that are easy to understand or follow, like stopping at a stop sign. Simple Rules are a complex phenomenon that coordinate individuals' behavior into complex interactions that becomes a *new* thing. Think about how often you'd wished for a way for individual people to act collectively so something new and powerful and beautiful could emerge. This is the process that leads to that outcome.

When enough individuals, grasshoppers or otherwise, start to follow the same Simple Rules, they are *self-organizing*. No design team, state-approved curriculum, or engineering plans required. They organize themselves, and, if there are enough individuals and energy, a whole new thing *emerges*. This complex phenomenon happens all around us all the time. It is the way the complex world works. No one designs COVID-19 variants. No one needs to. They emerge as the virus self-organizes and reorganizes.

Throughout their life cycle, complex systems, including humans and human societies, adapt, or learn, through self-organizing. Complex systems are layered networks that constantly sense feedback from their environment and seek information (differences that makes a difference). When systems sense a difference-making difference, they adapt, and new properties emerge (conveniently referred to as emergent properties).

Real learning is not memorizing what someone else already knows. Real learning generates (whole new) emergent properties. Although this is a very different way to think of learning than what the mechanistic paradigm teaches, new properties emerging through self-organizing is a common part of life. Think about washing your hands. Water is made up of two molecules of hydrogen and one molecule of oxygen.

Neither hydrogen nor oxygen is wet.

How is it then that water is wet when neither of the molecules that make up water is wet? Water is more than and other than the sum of its parts. Wetness is a new property that emerges when hydrogen and oxygen self-organize into water via a chemical reaction.

Let's keep washing our hands. How do we know where to hold our hands to get them under the faucet's flow? Depth perception. The late complexity scientist Gregory Bateson eloquently described how we perceive depth: "The binocular image, which appears to be undivided, is in fact a complex synthesis of information from the left front in the right brain and a corresponding synthesis of material from the right front in the left brain. Later these two synthesized aggregates of information are themselves synthesized into a single subjective picture from which all traces of the vertical boundary have disappeared.... We create new information about dimension as the information from both eyes interacts in our brains."

Learning is like wetness.

Learning is like depth perception.

Learning is like a locust swarm.

Learning happens when humans interact with their environment and the mind and body self-organize and reorganize, integrating new information from our experiences with information we've already organized, and from that process something new emerges.

Let's step away from the sink and go outside to see self-organized learning in action.

Do you remember learning to ride a bike? I do. I had a sparkly royal blue Schwinn with a white basket and handlebar tassels. Learning to ride was a big deal. My dad told me I could ride with him outside our neighborhood once I could handle my bike well on my own. I remember how disappointed I was at first when I couldn't keep both feet on the pedals. I had no awareness of the complex processes at play, but I knew my dad was there to hold the seat and help me steer until it all finally clicked.

What seems like an ordinary part of growing up is a massively complex exercise in self-organizing. When I learned to ride a bike, internal processes such as my sense of balance, desire to adventure with my dad, and coordination of muscle movement interacted with external sensations: the feel of my feet on the pedals, the sight of my fingers gripping the handlebar, the movement of air over my skin, the sound of the tires on the pavement. When vision and balance, muscles, and motivation all synced up to keep me and my sparkly bike upright and moving forward, that emergent property we call "riding a bike" happened because my neurons began to fire in a whole new (self-organized) way.

Bike riding, like depth perception, a locust swarm, and wetness, emerges as a whole phenomenon. Just as our brains form a whole image from both eyes, bike riding requires the rider to experience and sync up the relationships of all the moving parts.

Bike riding emerges whole.

You cannot learn to ride a bike from experiencing just the parts. You cannot learn to ride from pedaling an exercise bike or riding in a pedicab.

There is no way to learn to ride a bike without *riding* a bike.

Watching someone else ride a bike helped my brain begin the self-organizing process, but I didn't learn to ride a bike from watching my dad, reading about it, or memorizing what my dad told me to do. Ultimately, I learned by getting on the bike and engaging with the whole authentic complexity that is bike riding. All the relationships between all the actions and objects and internal and external information were experienced, connected, and exquisitely coordinated through self-organizing. That coordination required my neural pathways to reconfigure and create something whole and new: Look! Ida Rose is riding a bike!

A Whole New Way of Doing School

When we see learning in this whole new way, everything changes. We can't help but see that we need a whole new way of doing school. How do we get there?

By changing the Simple Rules.

Currently, the Rules of the Drill shape society and schools. Changing Simple Rules would change how we think and what we do. We can learn a lot about what Simple Rules are and how they allow whole new things to emerge from Dr. Iain Couzin, now the director of the Max Planck Institute of Animal Behavior in Germany. Dr. Couzin began his career at Princeton University, studying how lonely bugs become massive swarms. Swarm behavior is not small beans. Locust swarms can contain tens of billions of bugs and range from a fraction of a mile to a hundred square miles. In 2020, a plague of locusts descended on the Horn of Africa, threatening the livelihoods of 10 percent of the world's population. If we're interested in society shifting to a whole new way of doing school, we can learn a lot from the lowly grasshopper. Note that locusts' swarm behavior happens without a single locust being taught how to do it. No one raises money so grasshoppers can sit in classrooms and be schooled on how to consume massive amounts of food.

Swarms are not merely a group of grasshoppers hanging out for dinner. For a swarm to *emerge*, grasshoppers must not only gather in a sufficiently large group, but they all must also act in specific ways. Dr. Couzin, fascinated by the locust swarms he had observed in East Africa, equipped his Princeton lab with a large revolving disc (sort of like a round treadmill for bugs), high resolution video equipment, and a hefty supply of grasshoppers. He recorded hours of locust behavior. Through his research he learned that swarms emerge when grasshoppers follow four rules: (1) move quickly in the same direction as everyone else; (2) follow the bug before you; (3) bite slow-moving bugs; and (4) eat everything in your path, including the bug before you. In fact, his research showed that locusts move in the same direction to avoid being eaten by another locust. There you have it. Loner grasshoppers transformed into destructive swarms in four Simple Rules.

Over the last couple of decades, I've either led or collaborated on multimillion-dollar efforts to dramatically improve education. None of those efforts, however well-conceived, funded or implemented, have had anywhere near the effect that locusts had on the Horn of Africa in 2020. None of them have done anything to change the prevailing machine paradigm. Generation after generation, in conservative regions and progressive, both rural and urban, people have organized around the Rules of the Drill. Yes, great capacities have emerged, capacities to build great cities, send people into space, communicate globally. And also to do great harm.

Our global problems emerged from our current Simple Rules.

A vibrant future requires us to shift the Simple Rules.

What's Life Got to Do with It?

The whole new way of learning I propose resoundingly rejects the notion that we, our children, and our society are in any way, shape, or form machines. But if we're not machines, what are we? What is our role, our purpose on Earth? For now, let's go with this: Humans are infinitely complex, intelligent beings, *primarily responsible for making intelligent contributions to the continuation of life on Earth*.

If, fundamentally, humans are responsible for making intelligent contributions to the continuation of life on Earth, and schools are tasked with preparing young humans for this immense responsibility, before we can identify the Simple Rules we need for our planet to thrive and all beings to flourish, we first need a complex understanding of life.

I grew up seven minutes from San Diego's famous zoo. One of my greatest childhood joys was visiting and feeding the elephants (this was a thing at the time, but not now). I don't remember ever thinking an elephant was a dog, perhaps because I had more experience with pachyderms than canines. To this day, I can feel warm elephant breath on my palm as pudgy fingers at the end of bristly trunks scoop peanuts from my outstretched hand.

I also loved plants. Our backyard and my grandparents' backyard had lemons and figs and apricots and oranges and limes and tangerines. I loved picking and peeling the Meyer lemons. I ate them on the spot.

With all my love of plants and animals, you would think I loved biology. I didn't. I remember little from high school Bio 101, except the frog dissection. I nearly retched when the sorry fellow was laid out before me, but after my lab partner made her first slice and we pinned back the skin, I was captivated. There was so much going on under the surface. Everything inside the sacrificial creature looked like the drawings in our textbook. I was riveted by the idea that all that was going on under there could be known. I sensed the lesson wasn't just about the frog. It was about me and all other living things. So much was going on beneath the surface.

Looking back, I might have learned a great deal about life from freshman bio, but it was hot, I was distracted (by a boy), and the Aha! that connected frog guts with backyard lemons and zoo elephants slipped passed me as I did what was required to get a summer school A.

It also didn't help that neither the teacher nor the text taught that life is the wondrous link that exquisitely connects everything on Earth, nor as the most important concept we could possibly understand. Instead, both described life as a collection of characteristics with a long list of caveats: living things move on their own, except plants don't move—but they sort of do, here, watch this time lapse of a beanstalk growing. If the thing in question is an animal, then it breathes, land animals through lungs, water creatures with gills, except some water creatures have lungs. Viruses are confusing. They move on their own, but they are not alive because they need a host to reproduce. But so does mistletoe. So, is it alive?

It isn't surprising that high school bio in the mid-1970s used a complicated approach to teaching about life; at the time, there really wasn't a sufficient complex definition. In the early 1990s, top scientists on an advisory panel to NASA's astrobiology program decided a better definition was long overdue and proposed this one: *Life is a self-sustaining chemical system capable of Darwinian evolution*. Biophysicist Dr. Edward Trifonov thought that definition was cumbersome at best. So, in 2011 he analyzed 123 definitions of life and proposed one that is now generally accepted: *Life is self-reproduction with variations*.

That definition is worth several days' contemplation. Life isn't about locomotion or body parts, it's about *self-reproduction*. If you're thinking, "What in the world does that have to do with school?" please, hang in there. It has a *lot* to do with how we do school in a regenerative future.

Both the NASA and Trifonov definitions were based on the groundbreaking work of two renown biologists/neuroscientists from Santiago, Chile, Drs. Humberto R. Maturana and Francisco J. Varela. Maturana and Varela studied biological processes from a complexity perspective, much the same way we are considering learning through a complexity lens. In the 1970s, they coined a term to describe what they saw as the overarching characteristic of life: *autopoiesis* (auto-poi-EE-sis). The word is a combination of the Greek words auto, which means "self," and poiesis, which means "making." Thus, autopoiesis means "self-making" or "self-generation."

Maturana and Varela proposed that living systems organize themselves and their relationships with other things in their environment in ways that optimize their capacity for self-making. Defining life as process and relationships rather than a checklist of attributes has profound implications for how we live with one another and our planet and how we educate future generations. Later, in Chapter 7, we'll explore how humans learn from patterns. We'll see how exquisitely and intentionally infants do exactly what Maturana and Varela proposed. They interact with their environment in ways that optimize their capacity for self-making. They are absolutely not blank slates, *tabula rasa*, as philosopher John Locke long ago proposed.

When we truly start to understand wholeness and emergence and the relationship between everything and our own and others' self-making, we start to see how extraordinarily networked everything on Earth is and how those networks are the very nature of life. We thrive, individually and as a species, only when we participate intelligently and reciprocally in Earth's web of relationships.

Imagine what society would be like if the absolute need for *mutual thriving* was our fundamental paradigmatic assumption. When the prevailing worldview shifts to seeing the world and all living things as self-making entities living in networked ecosystems, we start to think in cycles; we start to see our place in the world and our responsibilities to the Earth and all that is in it in a whole new way, and we realize teaching young humans how to think with Regenerative Rules is the essential obligation of all parents, educators, and communities.

Let's ponder the notion of *organizing environments for self-making* in terms of the scenes and scripts of school. What might it look like if the scenes and scripts of school were intended to support young humans' autopoiesis, rather than the Rules of the Drill? Would we separate children by age? Or supposed ability? Would we slice and dice learning into grade levels and dole it out piecemeal according to a pacing calendar? What Simple Rules would set conditions for self-organizing for self-making and mutual thriving instead?

Regenerative Rules

I offer five simple Regenerative Rules, not as a doctrinaire set, but as a contribution to a way forward from industrialism to people and planet flourishing. You will notice that, like the Rules of the Drill, Regenerative Rules are Simple Rules for *thinking*. Unfortunately, human cognition in recent decades has gotten an undeserved bad rap, especially in educational circles. Yet paradigms and mental models, metaphors and stories—the stuff that has the potential to lead to societal change—are all artifacts of human cognition.

Thinking, which includes all human emotion and expressive movement, communication, relationships, and arts, is one of the most complex and powerful phenomena on the planet. It is also inextricably connected to change. Volumes of research across a variety of methodologies have demonstrated that changing thought changes emotions and behavior. Central to a regenerative approach to learning is a restoration of appreciation for the complexity and beauty of human cognition and how powerfully thinking affects not only our personal lives but society writ large.

Here I briefly introduce the Simple Rules. We'll use them in more depth throughout the remainder of the book.

Regenerative Rule #1: Think in Wholes

As I discussed earlier, thinking in wholes is thinking in complexity. The focus is on process and relationships. The *relationships* of parts to whole and whole to parts and parts to each other are more important than the parts. Thinking in wholes means we focus on phenomena that emerge from complexity that are greater than the sum of the parts (such as the wetness of water, depth perception, a child learning to ride a bike, or a societal shift to a regenerative paradigm).

Regenerative Rule #2: Think in Circles

Circles, and all their variations, such as spirals, waves, and cycles, are fundamental complex patterns. The closer a culture lives to the natural world, the more likely their people are to think in circles. Several years ago, a program officer at the US National Governors Association invited me to be a subject matter expert on educational assessment for an early childhood policy program they were running for six US states. I was assigned to support three states, including the team from Hawai'i, who were creating a policy statement on early childhood assessment for their governor's approval. About a month into the project, the National Governors Association staff member who was supporting the Hawai'i team called me in a bit of a panic.

"Ida Rose, I need some help. The Hawai'i team, um, they want their policy statement to *be in a circle*."

I smiled. "Of course they do," I said.

After a moment of silence, he replied, "I don't know how to do that."

"That's okay. They do."

When you start to think in circles, you start to wonder about cycles and how cycles might change with scale (cycles changing with scale are spirals), and you will find yourself uncomfortable with linear thinking and will start asking all kinds of questions, silently or aloud, that straight-line data simply can't answer, like, "How will this scholarship program amplify hardships for those who don't qualify?" or, "How will we set up intentional feedback loops?"

Regenerative Rule #3: Think Dynamically

Nothing is static. So, educational approaches that help humans learn how the world actually works aren't static either. Regenerative education immerses people in experiences and environments that are regularly changing, moving, and adapting. What kinds of environments are like that? Your typical classroom? I'm thinking not so much. Take a few minutes and try to imagine environments that are regularly in flux. I'm not talking about changing classroom bulletin boards, I'm talking about environments that evolve from sunup to sundown, that change as the weather changes, that host living species that interact with each other. What do they look like? Sound like? How can we use those imaginings to design regenerative learning environments that are regular experiences, not field trips or special classes?

Regenerative Rule #4: Think in Networks

Complexity happens within nested networks that quickly relay information throughout the system. Consider the Internet. Its nested networks quickly relay digital signals so that something happening in one part of the system registers almost instantaneously in millions of nodes, some thousands of miles away. The human nervous system is another. Even though our feet are far from the pain centers in our brain, a vast network of nested neurons lets us know immediately when we've stubbed our toe.

Self-organizing processes create connected networks that emerge from individuals and resources where the system is located. Thus, self-organizing processes custom fit complex systems to local conditions. Both biologists and developmental psychologists call that custom fit relationship an "ecological niche." With an origin process that generates a system from the peculiarities of a specific locale, the emerged system is highly sustainable, which is great if you want what emerged (such as a forest ecosystem, or a network of rural volunteer firefighters) and a disaster when you do not (such as COVID-19, or self-organizing vigilantes).

Regenerative Rule #5: Think Generatively

Generativity means setting conditions for emergence. That sounds fancy, but we do this all the time—every day, in fact. Every morning and evening during the growing season, I walk in my vegetable garden. I look at different things for each plant, but on every plant, I look for aphids. Aphids in a garden are like bacteria in my mouth. Under optimal conditions, they multiply faster than bunnies. Left unchecked, they will self-organize into a system that has capacities beyond each individual aphid becoming a large enough colony to destroy a plant. So, I take my walks, prepared to squish every aphid I find. If I see a lot hanging out together, I grab a hose with a good nozzle and spritz them. I am creating conditions that are inhospitable for them.

But I am doing more than that. I intentionally do not use methods that would create inhospitable conditions for their dreaded predator: the lovely little ladybug and their otherworldly-looking larvae. Although regular spritzing and squishing do a world of good, I am not in my garden every moment. I, and my zucchini, need the ladybugs. By leaving some aphids and taking care not to spritz off ladybug eggs or larvae, I set the conditions that aphid predators and my garden need to thrive.

The most critical task in regenerative learning is to set conditions conducive to life and learning. The task belongs to all learners (including those called teachers). Some conditions are physical, such as designing the space. Some conditions are temporal, such as the time of day, the length of engagement, or the season of the year. Many conditions are emotional. What kind of mood or aesthetic is most conducive to learning? What emotions are helpful to hold and exhibit during learning interactions?

Because emergence is at the heart of regenerative education, the primary conditions to be considered are generative, such as:

- What will learners experience that will support emergence of new ideas and learning?
- How will learners know when new learning has emerged?
- How will people in this learning space set conditions for emergence?

What Is Regenerative Education?

Regenerative education *calls us to return* to learning that is aligned and in harmony with the way the natural world works. In the edited volume *Regenerative Learning: Nurturing People and Caring for the Planet*, Satish Kumar, cofounder of Schumacher College in the United Kingdom and Editor Emeritus of *Resurgence & Ecologist*, describes regenerative schools like this:

> A good school is a community of learners where education is not predetermined by remote authorities, rather it is a

journey of exploration where students, teachers and parents are working together to discover right ways to relate to the world and to find meaningful means of living in the world.

Regenerative education is learning aligned with a regenerative worldview. A society shaped by a regenerative worldview prioritizes regenerating those aspects of human society that contribute to nurturing Earth and all Earth holds.

Dr. Daniel Wahl in his book *Designing Regenerative Cultures* poses three questions that introduce regenerative ways of thinking. I've tweaked the questions to situate them in the context of education:

1. How do we design [learning opportunities that support] the emergence of regenerative cultures everywhere?
2. How do we [design learning experiences that teach everyone how to] cocreate health, wellbeing, and happiness in thriving communities?
3. How do we [use education to] nurture human and planetary health [and] redesign the human presence on Earth?

In Part 2, I answer these questions with specific approaches to designing regenerative schools in the complex times in which we live.

PART II

Making Regenerative Schools Reality

6

Defining a Regenerative Paradigm

The present systems of education are fundamentally flawed and not fit for purpose.... We have to ask ourselves: why are we still giving the kind of education that has brought us to the precipice of disaster?
~ Satish Kumar & Lorna Howarth

I take comfort knowing I'm not the only parent whose kids had a problem with the flag poem. In her book *Gathering Moss*, Indigenous biologist and science writer Dr. Robin Wall Kimmerer recalls the day her sixth-grader's teacher called to say that Robin's daughter refused to pledge the flag and, awkwardly, other students had followed suit. The students were not disruptive. They sat silently while classmates stood for the recitation. Dr. Kimmerer's daughter justified her behavior saying, "Mom,... it's not exactly liberty if they force you to do it."

Right, kiddo, it isn't.

Yet coercion, in myriad shapes and flavors, shows up in schools around the globe all day, every day. Which speaks more loudly about the nature of pledging a flag, the words of the flag poem or the subtle coercion it takes to get children and adults all across the US to recite it every day?

Industrial society values compliance by people with less power with the desires of people with more power. Such expectations align with the complicated notion that certain outcomes are anticipated, given certain inputs. I flip a switch; the light turns on. I press a brake pedal; the car slows and stops. The light and the car *comply* with my desires. And hundreds of thousands of young people *comply* with their school's requirement that they stand, face a piece of cloth, put their hand over their hearts, and recite a poem that makes little sense to many and for many is not true. To question the irony of this mandate by those who live in the land of the free and the home of the brave is to invite condemnation.

Industrial capitalism needs people who comply with authority. Controlling people, things, and complexity is a primary goal of complicated systems. It is also one compelling reason many folks have a hard time working with complexity. We don't like the idea that we have zero control over it. Complication gives us at least the illusion of control, but even the illusion is temporary. If my leg tires of pushing the brake pedal, when I let up, the car will roll again. If the electrical grid fails, so will the light. Complicated coercion is exhausting. For everyone.

Productive, Respectful Citizens

To make industrial schooling attractive, compliance is marketed as teaching kids to be productive, respectful citizens, a notion central to the protestant work ethic that shaped colonialism and drives capitalism. It applauds those who are willing to labor for the benefit of someone who controls the resources they need to live. Being productive citizens requires that children and youth develop a compliant disposition and willingness to labor at least five days a week, week after week, month after month, year after year, for a lifetime, even if they do not like the work and are not motivated to do it.

The goal of education as we know it isn't for citizens to have the capacity to provide for themselves. The goal is for citizens to provide labor in such a way and at a low enough cost that a company can maximize profits, often for nonlaboring shareholders. In return, the company provides money to the laborer, and the laborer is responsible for providing for their needs with the money they earn. People who comply with the system and "live within their means" are considered upstanding members of society.

Satish Kumar says the silent part aloud: "If democratic societies are opposed to military dictatorship, then why should they embrace corporate dictatorship?" Yet this corporate-benefitting value system shows up in all sorts of educational spaces. While I was executive director of the Elementary Institute of Science in Southeastern San Diego, a wealthy philanthropist took particular interest in a project we wanted to launch that would have provided students a tuition-free course in computer coding equivalent to a two-year college degree. It was designed so that participating students would finish the course close to high school graduation. At other program sites, students who completed the course had been hired immediately after high school with annual salaries in excess of eighty thousand dollars (in 2015).

The philanthropist met with me several times, promising to donate funds to staff the program. After several meetings, with none of the promised funds donated, I accepted his request to meet again. Hoping to motivate him to move forward on his promise, I mentioned the salary range students could expect upon completion of the program. Instead of inspiring him, he wagged his finger in my face and said, "You've got to be careful with setting *those people* up to earn *that kind* of money. To be good employees, they need to feel *the lash of necessity*."

Gulp.

The students who would participate in the program were mostly from binational, immigrant Latino families. Gut kicked, I ended the meeting. It was abhorrent for a wealthy white man to think our students needed to feel any kind of lash and that he did not see empowering our kids to gain marketable skills as a good thing because it would undermine their willingness to comply with employers. I could conveniently dismiss his attitude as individual bigotry were it not something I've repeatedly encountered in educational settings. It's baked into the system.

Rarely does anyone question how capitalism structures the relationship between labor, employment, money, profit, and power. I grew up thinking this is just the way things work. I must work hard doing something I don't necessarily enjoy at a time and place decided by someone else to earn the money I need to live. Persons owning needed resources would control the relationship between my labor and the resources I could earn.

It didn't occur to me until I was well into midlife that this isn't the only way humans can live together. I had learned in school and in other social settings, of course, that democracy was sacred and communism was evil, with socialism trailing close behind. But beyond that, I was never engaged in thinking through what other options there might be. My guess is you weren't either.

More and more, as the very structure of industrial capitalism shows its frailty, people around the world are looking for other ways to live together. Many look to nature for clues about how we might live in more equitable and sustainable ways. That makes sense. We are nature, after all. In nonhuman nature, we find an entirely different story. Instead of coerced compliance, we find *reciprocity*. Instead of centralized hierarchy where a small number of individuals have an overabundance of resources and use that largesse to coerce others to produce even more, we find bountiful, reciprocal exchanges.

We exhale and the trees breathe in.

The trees exhale and we breathe in.

Species' needs are met, and they produce a yield. Those yields become a resource for others. Such reciprocity produces infinite sustainability. It renews, revives, refreshes, and regenerates. There is no need for coercion because all needs are met.

There is mutual thriving.

Our global problems emerged from our current ways of thinking.

Our current ways of thinking cannot solve them.

Regenerative Values

To regenerate means to renew or restore. Regenerative living is rooted in the notion that humans, as individuals, communities, and species, have taken more than Earth can give and have not renewed or restored Earth's resources. Regenerative living recognizes it is possible to live in ways that do not deplete Earth's resources, but we have failed to live in those ways. Therefore, we must not only refrain from depleting resources but we must also restore them. Regenerative living acknowledges that consumer lifestyles, rooted in industrial capitalism, are extractive and exploitive.

It is the opposite of regeneration.

We consume more than we contribute.

In the previous chapter I introduced Regenerative Rules, which are Simple Rules that are far more likely to set conditions for regenerative living than the Rules of the Drill. They are thinking tools that help us see complexity more clearly and act responsibly under conditions of high complexity. But regenerative living requires more than complexity thinking. Regenerative living is an approach to how we conduct our lives and raise our youth that is grounded in the values that emerge from our interconnection and interdependence with everything Earth holds. Habits of mind, like the Regenerative Rules, are necessary, but shifting society to a regenerative paradigm requires an entirely different ethical system than what industrialized capitalism values. For me, living a regenerative lifestyle means revering all beings, living in intentional reciprocity, and prioritizing mutual thriving.

Reverence

I glanced at the clock in the corner of my computer screen. We were already twenty minutes past our agreed-upon end time and had yet to get to the stated purpose of the meeting. Amid the COVID-19 pandemic, I was facilitating an international team of Human Systems Dynamics Professionals tasked with designing an online Open Space gathering to address the pressing needs of our rapidly changing world. Open Space was developed in the 1980s by Harrison Owen to help groups wrestle with complex issues. We, as the design team, had spent three two-hour meetings trying to articulate the theme that would frame the gathering. We had previously agreed that today, early in our meeting, we would finalize the theme and move on to pragmatics, specifically, how would we accommodate people living in all time zones? Instead, we had again spent the bulk of our time struggling to identify the Open Space theme. What did we really want people to grapple with?

Finally, we settled on *reverence*.

As frustrated as I was that we still hadn't solidified meeting times or figured out how to facilitate a global gathering, the time spent elucidating what we meant by reverence was worth it. I invite you to consider your own ideas of what the word means. My favorite definition comes from Dictionary.com: An attitude of deep respect *tinged with awe*.

Imagine schools based on deep respect tinged with awe, rather than coercion and efficiency. What if we revered children? What if teachers revered parents and parents held teachers in awe? What if the very core of the curriculum was reverence for oneself and one's self-becoming, and for one another, for Earth, and all Earth holds? Does reverence in this context or viewed this way feel weird to you? It did, at first, to me. But through those planning conversations and then the Open Space itself, I found myself embracing reverence as key to everything I hold dear. I now find myself immersed in reverence every day.

Yesterday I planted garlic. I broke apart each bulb and put a single clove into appropriately spaced holes in soil. I had four bulbs, yielding sixty cloves. Even if only 80 percent mature, those four bulbs will reproduce themselves twelve times over. These tasty, medicinal plants, under the right conditions, can create twelve times the amount of food I started with. As I held the cloves in my hand, I felt deep respect tinged with awe.

I *revered* the garlic.

I wanted to treat it well. To give it the conditions it needs to become all it can become. Come summer, I will harvest garlic that will provide food and medicinal benefits for many months. I will save the largest bulbs to plant in the fall. Each year the garlic will regenerate itself, and I will never buy garlic again. Reverence + Reciprocity = Regeneration. The new three Rs.

Reciprocity

In the 1970s, Bill Mollison and David Holmgren popularized a way of living and growing food called permaculture. If you're familiar with permaculture, you have likely recognized overlap between permaculture principles and what you're reading in these pages. Here I'll make a more explicit connection. A permaculture landscape places plants, animals, equipment, and buildings in such a way that yields from one element meet the needs of others. For example, ducks forage for food and need water not only for drinking but to dunk their heads so they can clear their nostrils and to help them digest food. In addition to eggs and (possibly) meat, ducks yield horrifically poopy water and world-class insulative feathers. Garden plots need water, nutrients, pest control, and mulch. In addition to food for ducks and humans, gardens yield a haven for bugs, which ducks love to eat. When ducks and garden plots are in close proximity to each other, the duck's poopy water can easily feed and water the garden, and their feathers can mulch the soil, conserving warmth and moisture.

The relationship between the garden and the ducks helps us properly understand reciprocity, for reciprocity is not merely collaboration. Fundamental to reciprocity is that everything involved gets what it needs. The trees breathe out and we breathe in. Ducks poop and veggies grow. Veggies attract pests and ducks fill their bellies. These reciprocal interactions benefit all. They support mutual thriving.

Without waste.

Reductionist, mechanical systems *separate* elements all in the name of efficiency. But separation doesn't create efficiency. It creates waste. Waste needs management. Management takes resources. It's all, sadly and ironically, extremely inefficient.

Like the education industrial complex, the food industrial complex also operates according to the Rules of the Drill. Industrial agriculture separates the fowl from the veggies. Poultry poop is waste that needs to be managed. Perhaps dumped in a sewer. Or harvested, bagged in plastic, transported via carbon-burning trucks and trains, and sold at big-box stores. Crops need pesticides because there are no ducks foraging for grubs. The yields of one element does not meet the needs of others because they are separated.

What does this have to do with education?

As you know by now, education as we know it separates children and sorts them into age groups. Yet any educator worth their credential will tell you that the best person to teach a child is another child, particularly an older child. They will also tell you the best way to learn something is to teach it. Do you see where I'm going with this? How could reciprocity work in regenerative schools? How did it work for millennia before industrial schooling?

Let's say a young child likes frogs. Who better to "teach" them about amphibians than an older child? And as that older child teaches her younger colleague, she learns too, on a deeper level. She makes play-by-play decisions about what's most important, decides how to organize experiences, and translates vocabulary for her younger companion. She's not only learning about frogs, but she's also learning how people learn and she's learning how *she* learns.

That sounds lovely. I want scenarios like this going on in schools all day, every day.

None of it can happen when eighth graders are forever separated from kindergarteners. When schools are structured so that there can be no reciprocity, children never learn to live reciprocally with others and with all beings. It cuts young humans off from one of the most important aspects of their humanity.

Regenerative schools change that.

Mutual Thriving

If we accept that humans are responsible for making intelligent contributions to the continuation of life on Earth and that humans' lifelong capacity to do that is indelibly shaped by their experiences in the first years of life, then schools must become the places where everyone has ample opportunity for self-becoming. Back in Chapter 5, I shared with you the work of Chilean biologists and philosophers Drs. Humberto Maturana and Francisco Varela. Their definition of life is at the heart of regenerative schools. In a regenerative paradigm where humanity's fundamental purpose is perpetuating life on Earth, supporting autopoiesis, self-becoming is central to schooling. In the words of Dr. Margaret Wheatley, "Autopoiesis is life's fundamental process for creating and renewing itself, for growth and change. A living system is a network of processes in which every process contributes to all other processes. The entire network is engaged together in producing itself. This process is not limited to one type of organism—it describes life itself."

Regenerative schools have the potential to be the nutrient-rich soil of autopoiesis. They would be hothouses of human capacity, cultivating all people's self-becoming. But education as we know it doesn't nurture self-becoming, and it hasn't since its inception. While I lived on Maui, there was a teacher strike, shutting down all schools across the state. The church where my family attended had classroom facilities that were vacant on weekdays. Several of us volunteered to provide learning-centered childcare so parents could continue working. I home-schooled my kids at the time, so I gathered all our cool, hands-on learning materials and volunteered for the math room in the morning and science in the afternoon.

On the first day, I spread out buckets of hands-on math equipment on a front table and showed everyone how to use them. There were no worksheets. No quizzes. Just lots of ways to learn fractions and geometry and algebra and trigonometry. My own kids worked alongside their friends, excited about math. Three *kupunas* (Hawaiian elders) volunteered to help. They quickly began balancing objects on the algebra scale and working through math puzzles with the Cuisenaire rods. Everyone had their hands on something.

I moved around the room, answering questions, loving how people of all ages were learning together. Then I noticed, as she focused on pattern blocks, one of the kupunas wiped a tear from her cheek. What? Oh no. I approached her and asked if everything was okay. She looked up. Her eyes were hard, her mouth drawn tight. Her voice belied her words.

"This is great! I'm having so much fun. I've learned things I never knew."

My brow furrowed. If her experience was so great, why the anger?

She continued, "Is this really math?" I assured her it was.

"Like, *real* math?" I assured her again it was.

"Why wasn't I ever taught *this* in school? Why wasn't I ever taught *like this* in school? I *hated* math. I thought I was horrible at it. Stupid, in fact. If *this* is math, why didn't they teach us math like this?"

At the time, I didn't know how to answer her. Now I would say, "Because learning and loving math are not the primary goals of schooling. Learning the Rules of the Drill is the primary goal."

A few months after the strike, I was in an adult Sunday School class in the same room. The class included several successful business owners. One of them, Bob, the owner of an island-wide soft drink franchise, was teaching. He asked how the church might help members of the Micronesian and Polynesian communities on Maui learn to be better employees, to be punctual, follow directions, and comply with employers' expectations. Bob, and the other businessmen, saw compliance as the way the Chuukese, Marshallese, Tongan, and Samoan immigrants could get and keep jobs.

I raised my hand. "Look at the wealth of expertise in this room!" I said. "You all know how to create and sustain viable businesses on Maui. Have you seen the Chuukese and Samoan weavings and textiles that they sell at the Saturday swap meet? Their skilled crafts are beautiful and I'm sure visitors would love to buy them, but the swap meet isn't marketed well. What if we ask what information, skills, and connections our brothers and sisters need in order to market their wares and help them create a small business incubator?"

I sat smiling, waiting for a robust discussion. Instead, everyone sat with eyes glued to their shoes. Bob cleared his throat. "First, they need to be good employees. That's how they'll learn to run a business."

I have no doubt Bob considered himself a benevolent champion of the Micronesian and Polynesian members of our community. But benevolence isn't a commitment to mutual thriving. Benevolence perpetuates the power imbalance inherent in industrial capitalism and poisons conditions for mutual thriving.

Just as the kupunas in my morning math class never had opportunities to thrive as mathematical beings, immigrants from other island nations weren't valued as fellow entrepreneurs fully capable of generating value for customers and for providing for their families and contributing to the community. They were only valued as workers who could fuel the prosperity of others.

None of this is mutual thriving.

Mutual thriving emerges from reverence and reciprocity. It is grounded in respect for others and the humble commitment to supporting everyone's self-becoming.

Yes, but How?

I hope as you read this chapter you find yourself longing to live in a world that prioritizes Regenerative Values. These values are that mark on the horizon we're longing for and (hopefully) moving toward. We've considered *why* a new paradigm is needed and *why* we need a whole new way of doing school in order to see the *what* emerge and to maintain it into the future. But *why* and *what* aren't enough. We need to know *how* we will get there.

Part 2 is all about the *how*. You won't find step-by-step recipes here. I've learned over the decades that prepackaged, recipe-like, canned approaches are embarrassingly impotent. If you spot red, green, and yellow dots next to children's names on a teacher's behavior reward chart, please know that someone somewhere is raking in the royalties for whatever prepackaged program the school bought. Any prepackaged approach, when it comes to creating regenerative schools, would be counterproductive. We need cohorts of people with deep capacity for applying complexity thinking and Regenerative Values to creating whole new schools.

There are several approaches to changemaking in complexity. I'll share the most practical and versatile one I've found. It's called Adaptive Action. Adaptive Action helps us find a way forward in the midst of complexity. Taking at least a tiny step forward, which is often the only thing we can do, opens up new perspectives and connects us with new information and relationships.

Adaptive Action is deceptively simple. It helps us make sense of complexity and to actively influence it. It helps us see the patterns underlying what appears to be chaotic. We can use Adaptive Action in our personal or professional lives, alone or with others. We can use it for designing large regional or even national systems, and we can use it with groups of ten-year-old children to help them direct their own learning.

You will benefit most from Part 2 if you create a "practice field" for experimenting with the ideas and approaches you'll learn. Your practice field can be a thought experiment or an actual situation. Think of it as a tangible way to practice some of the ideas in this section. Each chapter will include questions or suggested activities to help you imagine or actually plan how to take effective action in your practice field. Each chapter also ends with a summary and prompts to support your efforts. Don't worry if your imagined or actual project is small. An intergenerational garden at your child's preschool, a scout troop, or a book club exploring regenerative practices are great practice fields. Lots of small nodes, networked and sharing information and resources, are what generate tipping points in complex systems. Small is often the only viable path to complex change.

Adaptive Action: A Way Forward in Complex Systems

Adaptive Action was developed by Dr. Glenda Eoyang, who founded the field of Human Systems Dynamics and the Human Systems Dynamics Institute in Minneapolis, Minnesota. I love Adaptive Action because it is simple to remember, applicable to all complex situations, and remarkably effective when complexity has us flummoxed. As Glenda and her coauthor Royce Holladay write in their book *Adaptive Action: Leveraging Uncertainty in Your Organization*, "It is easy to become paralyzed by uncertainty." Adaptive Action is an iterative process that moves us through uncertainty to wise action.

I find Adaptive Action useful because it focuses us on *adapting* rather than solving or fixing, and because it prompts us to *action*. It recognizes at the onset that whenever we're stuck in complexity, we need to adapt, and that adaptation requires that we get past admiring the problem and act. Adaptation may seem obvious in the face of complexity, but how often have you been involved in intentionally thinking through how to *act* adaptively? One of the required courses in my educational psychology Ph.D. program at the University of Arizona was called Seminal Readings and was taught by our department chair. We read a large sampling of the educational psychology research literature of the past fifty years or so. For each lengthy article or chapter, we had to write a paper with two sections: What? (a brief description of the research discussed in the article) and So What? (a discussion of why the research mattered). I learned a lot and enjoyed the intellectual challenge, but I always felt like something was missing.

Now I know. Action was missing.

Even the most profound research findings are nothing more than intellectually interesting if they are not actionable. Adaptive Action has three phases: What? So What? and Now What? The last phase prompts us to action.

To get started with Adaptive Action, please take a few minutes to write a brief description of your practice field. This will start your What? phase. You can do this individually or with others. Imagine waving a magic wand and two years from now an entirely new school (as defined previously) has emerged. Describe that. You're just dipping your toes in this process. Don't take a lot of time, but write a solid, one-paragraph description with enough detail that someone else could envision it. Use words that conjure vivid imagery and awaken your emotions. Slow down enough to feel what you're imagining. If you're working in a group, I suggest having each person write a description. There's no need to come up with a single joint description at this point. Keep your description handy as we go through the three Adaptive Action phases, and take notes about anything that sparks your curiosity.

Adaptive Action Phase 1: What?

In the What? phase, we describe the situation we're wanting to influence and identify and name patterns. We're going to spend all of Chapter 7 defining patterns and exploring why they're important. For now, it's important to understand that human brains automatically perceive, derive meaning from, and respond to patterns, that's why most patterns fly under the proverbial radar. Humans can hold an infinite amount of information in long-term memory, but our working cognition is very limited. In psychology, we call the thoughts, emotions, expectations, or values that operate outside our conscious awareness *implicit* and those in our conscious awareness *explicit*. We can only hold about seven bits of information in our conscious, explicit awareness at a time. With such a limited capacity for holding explicit information, much of what goes on in our minds happens outside our awareness and thus outside of our ability to act intentionally.

For example, I knew, intellectually, that the place on the horizon where the sun rises and sets changes with the seasons. But it wasn't until I became a serious grower of food that I truly noticed seasonal changes and the patterns became meaningful. I started to collect data on how many hours of daylight each of my raised beds received and to notice where sunlight fell on the hardscape of our back patio, reflecting heat and light on the fruit trees. These data helped me understand how my backyard microclimate affected my plants and to take action to increase my yield, such as adding shade cloth at certain times of the day and adjusting irrigation schedules. My implicit knowledge became explicit when the complex patterns I was immersed in were relevant to something I cared about. Adaptive Action helps make *implicit* patterns *explicit* and helps us see their relevance. When complex patterns are explicit, we can intentionally act to adapt rather than merely react when we're caught off guard.

In the What? phase, we collect data about the issue, situation, or phenomena we're trying to address. Play with this phase by thinking beyond the description of your practice field and brainstorming some of the patterns that affect what you've imagined for the future. Who would be excited about what you've imagined? How would they express their excitement? Who would not be excited, and why wouldn't they be? What patterns would contribute to making your imagined future a reality? What would get in the way? Don't worry about being right or capturing all your thoughts. Just get the ball rolling.

Adaptive Action Phase 2: So What?

So what? is the meaning-making phase. Let's think about our toddler friend, Aisha from Chapter 2. Aisha was trying to make meaning out of her encounter with an elephant. After all the affirming reactions she got when she pointed at the family pup and said, "Doggy!" suddenly her uncle messed with meaning. Aisha had options. She could be curious. Why was her beloved uncle telling her that the big gray "doggy" was not a doggy? She could acquiesce. Sure Uncle, it's not a doggy, it's an elephant. Whatever you say! Side note: even though acquiescence passes as learning all the time, it isn't. Or Aisha could do what she did, which was to hold on tightly to the meaning she possessed. Doggy! This is how people typically respond when new experiences challenge something they believe to be true.

To make meaning in complexity, we need to hold loosely that which we believe to be true. The So What? phase can be a safe container for us, individually and collectively, to play with ideas that challenge meaning. It's the phase where we consider how we might expose ourselves to challenging ideas. In So What? we make meaning by carefully and candidly examining the data we collected in the What? phase and we begin to generate options for action that we then consider more deeply in the Now What? phase.

Think about how you might gather information that can help you understand your patterns for your practice field. For example, maybe you want to create an intergenerational learning program in a local public park. You could go to that park for thirty minutes at different times on different days and take notes about who's there and what they're doing. What patterns did you observe? Why might those patterns matter? What might they mean? What patterns might you be overlooking? Who could help you see patterns you're not seeing?

Identify how you might gather information about the patterns that affect your practice field. Remember, you're not trying to get it right. You're just dipping your toes in the process.

Adaptive Action Phase 3: Now What?

Think of Adaptive Action as a spiral where the first cycles are small and short, perhaps taking just an hour or two. As more information is gathered and as you, individually or collectively, get a better understanding of the relevant patterns, and you return again and again through the three phases, the spiral widens, encompassing more information, usually more and better questions, and perhaps more people. After making patterns explicit in the What? phase, and then making meaning of those patterns in the So What? phase, you're ready to identify wise action.

In early iterations of Adaptive Action, the Now What? phase often yields a few smallish actions while simultaneously pointing back to starting over again with the What? phase. Maybe you need to interview someone or gather data from the Internet to better inform the next What? phase. Or maybe you identify someone who should be part of the process and need to invite them before starting the next Adaptive Action cycle.

Expect the actions in the first few Adaptive Action cycles to be few and small. Please write that on a piece of paper and hang it somewhere you can see it often: *few and small*. The biggest mistake people make with early rounds of the Now What? phase is thinking they need to articulate a two-year plan with five strategies and tactics for each. Nope. That's not what Adaptive Action is about. Now What? is about identifying the *next* wise action. Set aside any pressure you may feel to come up with a Big Idea or to lay out a strategic plan. To move wisely and effectively in complexity we must learn to walk incrementally, recognizing that each step, each small difference, can take us on an entirely new trajectory. Adaptive Action is a powerful method because it can move both slowly and quickly and adapt to changing circumstances. Often, the next wise action is to simply start again.

Or take a nap.

Or eat lunch.

Naps and lunch might not seem very "productive" and yet taking a break is often exactly what people need. When I was in a governing board meeting of the National Association for the Education of Young Children in Washington, DC, we were circling around a controversial issue, stuck between opposing opinions. Unfortunately, the confines of Robert's Rules of Order make it difficult to break such a stalemate. I asked to be recognized. "I'm in desperate need of a bio break but I don't want to miss such a robust discussion. Could we break for ten?" The break was granted. As people used the facilities or grabbed a cup of tea and some snacks, mini conversations broke out in the meeting room and the ladies' room. In these informal conversations, people clarified concerns, identified places of agreement, and came closer to understanding points of difference all while washing hands or grabbing tea. When we returned, the conversation became productive and yielded a next action.

The lesson? Breaks aren't a waste of time. They're essential to complex work. They're a legitimate answer to the Now What? phase. Breaks allow our wondrously complex brains to relax and reorganize our thinking. Use them liberally.

CHAPTER SUMMARY

Key Points

1. Regenerative Rules are complex Simple Rules for thinking in ways that allow regenerative phenomena to emerge. They are necessary but insufficient for regenerative schools. Regenerative schools need to be grounded in regenerative values.
2. I propose three Regenerative Values:
    - Reverence
    - Reciprocity
    - Mutual Thriving
3. Adaptive Action is an iterative approach to figuring out how to act wisely under conditions of high complexity.
4. Adaptive Action has three phases:
    - What? The description and pattern-finding phase
    - So What? The meaning-making phase
    - Now What? The next wise action phase

Playing with Complexity

Individually or with others, explore your What? more deeply. Here are some questions that are especially helpful in the What? phase:

- What are ways that we can ensure Reverence, Reciprocity, and Mutual Thriving show up in our efforts? What other Regenerative Values do we want to commit to?
- What are some good examples of what we're dealing with or hope to accomplish?
- What would things be like in three years if what we want comes to fruition?
- What obstacles do we face?
- What resources are available to us? What assets do we already have on board?
- What patterns in the people, places, ecosystems, rules/regulations, mindsets, or other areas are important for us to pay attention to and learn more about?
- What are we missing? What are we not perceiving, and what could we do to improve our perception?

7

People, Patterns, and Expertise

Patterns are similarities, differences, and connections that have meaning across space and time.
~ Dr. Glenda Eoyang

Why do our schools teach us nothing about the pattern which connects?
~ Gregory Bateson

The door to my office was flung open, and Beth, a fourth-grade teacher entered and gingerly closed the door behind her. I looked up. Beth breathlessly tried to gain her composure.

Something must be horribly wrong.

"I need your help," she said.

Now I *knew* something was horribly wrong. Beth and her fourth-grade colleagues had made it clear when I joined the school's faculty that they did not need a school psychologist. They handled all student and classroom matters themselves. Yet here was Beth, catching her breath, asking for help.

"Marian, you know, that lovely child from that lovely family..." she started. I didn't know Marian or her family. Beth caught her breath again and continued, "Marian came to school this morning sobbing because—oh I just can't believe it—her father left the family! Such a lovely family. I can't believe it. How could he?" Beth pulled a tissue from the cuff of her sleeve and dabbed her eyes. "What am I going to do?"

My parents divorced when I was in fourth grade, so the depth of this teacher's concern touched me. But I was also puzzled. Why did this teacher assume *she* needed to *do* something?

I contemplated possible responses and landed on my favorite: *ask the child.*

"Where is Marian now?"

Beth glanced at the clock above my door. "She's at recess. She only completed half her morning work. I'm afraid she's going to come in after recess and be a distraction." This teacher clearly cared for Marian. She also cared about running an orderly classroom.

"When recess is over, just send Marian to me," I offered. "I'll send her back once she's calmed down, and I'll give her mom a call, so we know how to best support the family."

Beth smiled, thanked me, and left. Five minutes later, a red-faced Marian peeked inside my door. I invited her to sit at my conference table and closed the door behind her.

"Your teacher is concerned about you and asked me to talk with you. Is that okay?"

Marian nodded. "I just don't know how I'm going to…" her voice broke.

"When did you find out your dad was leaving?"

She sniffed hard. "Last night! And then this morning he left as we were eating breakfast."

I tilted my head. Something in the story sounded "off." Maybe dads leave "lovely" families differently than the family I grew up in, but really? Just say goodbye and leave in the middle of your young kids' Monday morning breakfast?

Again, *ask the child* came in handy. "What bothers you about your dad leaving?"

The dam burst. "What if he dies? What if his plane crashes? What if I never see him again?"

Ahh. Okay. Maybe daddy isn't *leaving* the family. I began to form hypotheses based on patterns I'd observed with children over the years. Maybe this is separation anxiety over a trip her dad is taking.

"Those worries sound scary. Where did your dad go?" I asked.

Marian wiped her nose with the tissue I offered. "Houston. I think."

Family therapists are trained to form hypotheses about a client's situation but to hold those hypotheses lightly and be ready to revise them as new information reveals itself. For me, when new information seems to confirm my hypotheses it's like a bell goes off in my mind, confirming the pattern (and a buzzer sounds when it doesn't).

"Does he travel a lot?" I asked.

Marian nodded. *Ding*.

"And you really miss him when he goes."

She nodded again. *Ding. Ding*.

"When is he coming back?"

"Friday."

"Okay, so today is Monday. He'll be gone four nights?"

"Next Friday," she said. Ah, too long for this child. Just too long.

"Oh. So, he's gone for a longer trip than usual?"

Marian nodded. *Ding. Ding. Ding*.

I got up, took my calendar off the wall and put it on the table. "Let's count how many days until he comes home." Together we counted.

"Sometimes when I'm waiting for something important to happen, it seems like forever, so I play little games with myself to make the time go by more quickly. Would you like to try a game?" I asked.

Marian smiled weakly. "Sure."

"Okay, how about this." I grabbed some colored paper and scissors. "Let's cut some paper strips and you can write something you love to do with your dad on each one. Then we'll make a paper chain. Each night you can take one of the links off the chain and either tell him about it when he calls you, our leave it for him in a special place for when he gets home."

Marian's eyes lit up. We cut the paper, she wrote on each strip, and we put the chain together.

"Are you ready to go back to class?" I asked.

Marian nodded.

"How about you first go to the restroom and wash your face. Smile at yourself in the mirror and tell yourself it's going to be okay. Then come back and get your chain."

Marian smiled a real smile and headed to the restroom. She came back, grabbed her chain, and walked to her classroom.

Forty-five minutes later, at the start of lunch, Beth showed up at my door. "What in the world did you do to that girl? Did you work some kind of magic? She came back smiling, happy, saying her dad was on a business trip, and showing everyone her paper chain. I don't know how you did that. I couldn't get her to stop crying. Thank you."

I loved helping an upset child and her teacher, but what I did wasn't particularly inspired, much less magic. Even though I had only been a school psychologist a few years, I had first been trained as a family systems therapist, and that training immersed me in complexity thinking. I came to understand children as complex beings living in complex family systems, which are nested in complex systems of communities and society. Whatever is going on with children emerges from the complex patterns at play in *all* those nested, networked systems, not just from within the child.

When you develop expertise in complex patterns and the Simple Rules that influence them, responding to just about any emotionally fraught circumstance becomes manageable and at times even magical.

Complex Pattern Expertise: What It Is, How We Develop It, and Why It Matters

What feels like magic is, in reality, the human capacity we call expertise. Our complicated educational system has led us to believe expertise is simply accumulating knowledge, and to ensure no one claims expertise illegitimately, expert knowledge is codified in academic degrees and professional credentials.

But true expertise isn't merely an accumulation of knowledge. Expertise is acquired by being repeatedly immersed in experiences that expose us to specific patterns that we then internalize. During the internalization process, the brain forms neural pathways that allow us to immediately recognize patterns and simultaneously attach meaning to those patterns and know how to respond. Internalization is why the scripts and scenes children experience at school are so potent. Children internalize the patterns associated with separating, sorting, and sequencing day after day, year after year. They become experts in the Rules of the Drill well before age ten. Changing to regenerative Simple Rules in schools means learners internalize the patterns that go with wholes and cycles, generativity, and networks.

Internalizing patterns is the most powerful way humans learn, and we do it without ever cracking a textbook. A friend recently told me about how her husband, Dan, a heavy equipment operator, once saved several coworkers from serious injury or death. He was excavating a trench in an unusually sandy job site. His coworkers had gained their limited experience in northern Arizona where the soils are primarily heavy clay. Dan, who had worked in lots of different places including many with sandy soil, was working on an excavating machine when he turned around and saw that the trench his coworkers were in was unstable and about to collapse. He yelled at them to get out of the trench. They did, just before it crumbled. None of his inexpert coworkers recognized that the sandy soil was unstable. But Dan did. He had expertise from internalizing the complex patterns he had experienced from years of working in a variety of soils.

When Dan turned and saw his coworkers in that trench, he saw patterns that indicated imminent collapse. Collapse, as we'll see later in this chapter, is a common complex pattern. Over the years and with hundreds of previous experiences, Dan had internalized what stable patterns look like and what collapse patterns look like. I haven't asked Dan, but I would bet good money he would likely not be able to articulate the specifics of the patterns he saw that alarmed him. *He just knew*. On the morning I helped Marian, I don't think I could have described what I did. *I just knew*. Expertise doesn't come about from accumulating knowledge. It comes from being immersed in experiences and *internalizing* (organizing and reorganizing) the patterns associated with those experiences. We often can't describe exactly why we did what we did because most patterns are nonverbal.

Experience is crucial for developing expertise because as humans we innately sense and make sense of patterns and internalize that meaning, often in nonverbal ways. This is why the Rules of the Drill have been so successful. From a very young age, we have internalized separateness as *normal*. Imagine what the world would be like if the vast majority of the world's humans had internalized thinking in circles and cycles and generativity from the earliest years of their lives. The nonverbal experiences that we immerse children in for their first two decades of life are immeasurably important because humans begin internalizing patterns even before birth and use patterns expertly even before we can walk or talk.

People Are Born Pattern Experts

Humans are born with an innate capacity for developing pattern expertise. If you are an early educator or developmental specialist, you know how adept infants and toddlers are at learning complex patterns. If you are not familiar with early human development, it may surprise you to learn that without any formal instruction, human babies sense and make sense of myriad complex patterns. This sensing and sense-making happens because the human brain, the most sophisticated of complex system humans know of, interacts with complexity and then organizes itself around the environmental stimuli it receives.

At birth, human brains begin identifying which neural pathways fire most often. The brain preserves neurons that fire most frequently, and those that don't fire die off. The neurons in the pathways that remain sync up with nearby neurons, forming even stronger neural pathways.

One of the most awe-inspiring examples of how humans develop expertise is how babies learn language. I always find it disorienting to see a newborn foal, just moments after birth, push up and stand on its spindly legs. How do they do that? But human babies, with all their relative immobility, do something far more remarkable. Typically developing babies become experts in their family's language with no formal instruction. Let's briefly explore how babies learn language "on the fly" because it gives us a template for understanding our own innate ability to develop expertise from being immersed in complex patterns.

Babies immersed in a language-rich environment use it as a linguistic practice field. They develop language expertise from hearing words *they do not understand*. That's a big part of the complexity-learning template: *humans develop pattern expertise from being immersed in complex patterns before we understand them*. When it comes to learning language, the most important thing parents and other caregivers can do is talk and sing—a lot! That's because even the youngest child is keenly sensing and remembering the patterns in the human voices they hear.

Developing this kind of expertise happens "under the radar." During the process, we are usually completely unable to demonstrate our expertise or even give an indication we're paying attention, until what we've been learning emerges whole. Our brains observe and organize and reorganize and self-organize and then, seemingly overnight, something new emerges—like riding a bike, or responding effectively to a distraught fourth grader, or recognizing imminent collapse of a trench.

A critical part of that organizing and reorganizing includes identifying what to keep and what to toss. Humans are born with an immeasurable number of nerve cells (called neurons) and continue to overproduce an abundance of them for about three years. Like a prolific, unruly tomato patch, this overabundance of neurons needs to be pruned into the high-capacity pattern organ that is the adult human brain. A few decades ago, scientists believed that human development was merely a series of prepackaged DNA-driven milestones unfolding that were only minimally affected by the child's experiences. With advances in neuroscience, we now know that the patterns infants experience in their environment profoundly affect the way they sense their world and make sense of it. Their early experiences actually *shape their brains* through a process called *synaptic pruning*.

Our ability to make sounds is a great example of synaptic pruning. Babies are born with the neurons they need to produce *all* the vocal sounds that humans make. I'm not talking about just vowels and consonants, but *all* human sounds. I grew up in a bilingual home. I always knew who my mom was talking to on the phone by the mix of Sicilian and English she spoke. If it was my grandmother, it was nearly all Sicilian. If it was my aunt, about half and half. If it was my uncle, mostly English. One thing everyone in my family did was say goodbye using the formal *arrivederci*, rather than the casual *ciao*. As children, we did the same. From toddlerhood, I have been able to roll an r like a native Sicilian speaker. So can everyone in my family. But none of us can make the clicking sounds used in the Khoisan languages of Africa. I had the capacity to make those sounds at birth. So did you. But because we did not use those sounds in the first few years of life, those neural pathways died off.

This language example illustrates another big part of the template for how humans develop pattern expertise by being immersed in complexity: we do not develop expertise in those complex patterns that we're not immersed in. Children spending their first decade or more being immersed in the Rules of the Drill is, of course, problematic. But what is far more problematic is that they are not immersed in the Regenerative Rules. Thinking in complexity does not become internalized, and we find ourselves in adulthood wondering why so much of what we try to do to affect change just yields bucketloads of Unintended Consequences. All this means that for those of us raised in industrial education, we need to intentionally immerse ourselves in complexity even if we're not yet sure what it all means. It means developing practices such as standing outside with our eyes closed and focusing on the feel of the wind on our bodies. It means listening intently to a mockingbird in spring. Can we hear the distinct patterns in all the different songs it sings?

Let's think again about how babies develop complex pattern expertise. How do infant brains know which neurons to keep and which to prune? The fascinating work of Dr. Alison Gopnik, a developmental psychologist at University of California, Berkeley, gives us some clues. Through some clever experiments, she and her research team demonstrated that infants use statistics and distinguish between language sounds they hear at a statistically higher frequency and those they hear less frequently. To know which sounds to keep, young children, from infancy, need lots and lots and lots of exposure to language patterns. It's so important, they instinctively seek pattern information. Think about how babies interact with adults. They babble and coo and smile. They're downright flirts. We're all enamored. Those big eyes! And then they smile and pass a bit of gas. Oh my! Adorable. They're cute for a reason. When babies flirt, what do we do? We pick them up and *we talk to them*. How do we talk and what do we say? Do we tell babies financial news or rant about politics? No. We make exaggerated silly faces, and *we talk baby talk*. Baby talk is a distinct language pattern in which the speaker emphasizes certain sounds. Listen closely to baby talk. Vowel sounds are elongated. It's singsong-y. Baby talk amplifies what the child should pay attention to.

At about one year of age, after babies have been sampling language sounds for hundreds of days, most children say their first word. First words emerge when children's brains have reconfigured the complex information they've heard for the past year into something entirely new. For first words to emerge, the sound pattern must *mean* something. First words are an indication that the child understands that spoken words represent something.

From months of exposure to patterns that initially have no meaning, babies have the innate ability to recognize the relationship between those patterns and things in their environment.

Understanding the relationship between language and object is the first step toward deriving meaning from language.

If I were writing this passage as an early childhood advocate, I would now pivot to make a policy argument for investing in early childhood education. But that is not the point of this chapter. The point of this chapter is not that young humans' development is most malleable in the first three to five years of life. (It is.) The point is not that young children benefit immensely from daily exposure to an abundance of language stimuli. (They do.) The point is that *we drastically underestimate the capacity we all have to recognize and make meaning of complex patterns, and that meaning-making in complexity comes from being immersed in it even when we don't yet understand it.*

The only way to evolve our ability as individuals, as communities, as societies, and as a species to live well with increasing complexity is to regularly engage with it. The trouble is that high levels of complexity are confusing. The complexity learning curve, even though we all went through it as infants, is uncomfortable. We might feel stupid. It doesn't make sense. And we are impatient. We want answers now, and complexity learning can take a long time. But it isn't just young humans that need regular exposure to incomprehensible levels of complexity. *All* humans need such exposure so we can expand our capacity for recognizing and influencing complex patterns.

If we want to create schools where young children expand their innate capacities for complex thinking, we, as the adults with the power and resources to make educational change happen, must immerse ourselves in complex patterns even if they don't yet make sense. To that end, in the remainder of this chapter, you'll find a complexity pattern primer. A primer, by definition, is merely an introduction. Entire books have been written about complexity and the kinds of patterns it creates. My intention here is to give you enough of an introduction that you can start looking for complex patterns in your everyday life.

I can point out the patterns, but you need to jump in the deep end yourself.

Complex Patterns: A Primer

As discussed above, humans have tremendous capacity to know what complex patterns are, recognize them in our daily lives, anticipate how they will behave, derive meaning from them, and use them to set conditions conducive to life. However, one of the tricky things about complex patterns is that we often can't see them. Changing perspective helps. When I'm stuck in parking-lot-like traffic on a ten-lane Southern California freeway, I can't see what's causing the delay. But the helicopters flying overhead can. Having a collection of pattern models can help us change our perspective and give us a bird's-eye view of the patterns we're dealing with. They can help us recognize, understand, and influence patterns that we might not otherwise discern. However, as Dr. George Box, the British statistician, famously said, "All models are wrong. Some are useful."

Dr. Box was speaking about statistical models, but the observation holds for all models. I'm about to share several models of complex patterns. As Dr. Box said, they are all wrong. That's okay. Because they are also useful.

Indulge me a digression.

Have you been to LEGOLAND in Carlsbad, California? I'm not a huge fan of amusement parks, but LEGOLAND is a ton of fun. On one ride, reminiscent of Disney's It's a Small World, patrons ride in automated boats down a winding canal around models of famous landmarks such as India's famous mausoleum, the Taj Mahal, all built out of LEGO. When conducting complexity thinking workshops, I often show a picture of the LEGOLAND version and ask attendees what it is. Inevitably, someone shouts, "The Taj Mahal!"

I respond, "Not quite! It is a *model* of the Taj Mahal, and it's *wrong*!"

It's wrong in many ways.

It's only three feet tall.

It's made of plastic.

It's not in India. It's in Southern California.

The proportions are way off, and I'm sure there are myriad other ways it is wrong. But you get the point. The model is *wrong*. But it is also *useful*. It helps us know what the real Taj Mahal looks like and can spark useful conversations about India, its culture, and its people, about death and wealth.

Like the LEGOLAND Taj Mahal, the pattern models I share in this chapter are, at least in some ways, wrong. They are also useful. Think of them as metaphors that help bring the abstraction of complex patterns into clearer conceptual focus. At the same time, remember their limitations. For example, complexity never shows up as just one pattern. Complex patterns overlap and constantly change. Also, I group patterns into change patterns, flow patterns, and structural patterns. That grouping is arbitrary. Many patterns fit into more than one category, and I'm sure other people would identify more categories or group pattern types differently. Hold these pattern models loosely. The goal isn't precision. The goal is perception. The more you start to see complex patterns in your everyday life, the more capacity you will have for influencing them.

Structural Patterns

When complex systems form, they self-organize into "structures." Complex system structures are not like what we normally think of as a structure. We usually think about structures as buildings or bridges. But complex structures take myriad shapes and sizes. A tree is a complex structure. So is a baby. Having expertise in the structural patterns that make up systems helps us know how to influence them. There are an unlimited number of complex system structures, but you need to develop expertise in at least these three: swirls and cycles, networks, and fractals.

Swirls and Cycles

The second Regenerative Rule, introduced in Chapter 5, is Think in Circles because circularity is one of the primary ways complexity moves. Earth rotates on its axis and revolves around the sun. The moon revolves around Earth. That movement creates all kinds of circular patterns in nature. Dust devils, tornadoes, hurricanes, and cyclones are all examples of how Earth's rotation shows up in our lives. We're all familiar with the circle of life, often depicted as the transformation of a caterpillar into a butterfly. Seeing in circles, thinking in circles, and acting to affect circles helps disrupt linear thinking. It also helps us think in terms of causal loops (see flow patterns), which helps us identify where in complex systems our actions will have the most influence.

Networks

As we'll discuss in much more depth in Chapter 8, complex systems are comprised of connected individuals. The importance of recognizing networks cannot be overstated. Failing to see and understand the connectedness of everything and acting as if decisions we make about children and schools happen in isolation is the root cause of unwanted, Unintended Consequences. As I described in Chapter 5, being able to think in networks is critical because networks disperse resources and create redundant essential functions, which contributes to the resilience of complex systems.

Fractals

A fractal is a pattern that repeats at different scales. Look closely at a tree and you'll see that the branch pattern repeats itself—it's larger at the base and smaller near the top. Look at a snail shell, or a succulent, or a crystal. Nature is full of fractals. Fractals display self-similar patterns, though not exact replicas, at different scales.

When you start seeing fractals in nature, it's easier to spot them in complex human systems. Recognizing fractals as a complex pattern reminds us to consider the most effective scale to try to influence, and it also reminds us that the patterns we're dealing with at one level are likely to be present at other levels.

Flow Patterns

Complexity moves. The gravitational pull of the sun moves planets in orbits, and the way Earth formed started it spinning. Those movements make air move as wind and water move as waves. Some flows we can see, such as water in a river or traffic on a freeway. Others are either hard or impossible to see, such as information flowing through an organization or fear moving through a fourth grader whose father is on a business trip. Understanding flow patterns helps us consider how information or energy is moving in complexity and how we might influence it. There are many important flow patterns, but for our purposes, let's explore two: sinks (sometimes called checks) and causal loops.

Sinks and Checks

Where I live, there is no municipal water supply and it is way too expensive to drill for a well (the aquifer is several thousand feet deep), so everyone hauls water from a few private wells, or harvests rainwater from rooftops. Another way to capture rainwater and snow melt is via passive rainwater catchment. There are many passive rainwater catchment techniques. One method is to create a check dam, which doesn't block water, but slows water enough for it to sink into the ground.

Water isn't the only thing that flows in complex systems. Ideas, energy, information, resources, power, and assistance also flow. The list is endless. Sinking happens at both the societal and individual levels. The information that Aisha's uncle was trying to share with her hit a big check dam when Aisha insisted the elephant was a dog. Her uncle noticed the check and came back with more information. Sometimes this is a good approach, but often, especially when systems are learning (see more in Chapter 10) it's better to let information sink in. When people (or large systems) are learning, the "sinking in" process is much more complex than water replenishing an aquifer. The system must reconfigure itself to adapt to new information or resources.

This is a common phenomenon with young children learning more than one language. As they gain new words, concepts, or syntax, they speak a lot less for a while. It isn't a language delay. Their brain is reconfiguring, which takes time and repeated exposure. The lag time between actions and outcomes can be very disconcerting for those of us who are accustomed to cause and effect being close in time and space. During a sink process, it can seem like our efforts have just disappeared. They've just been swallowed whole. Poof! Gone. But they're not. They're doing the complex work we need them to do.

Sink patterns are one reason why school reform doesn't work. Nearly all school reform is funded with short turnarounds—a year, maybe two. When the system (a school, classroom, district, or regional educational system) doesn't respond as anticipated within the timeframe, funds usually stop flowing. Reforms almost always fail to allow enough time for the system to learn.

Causal Loop

Causal loops are hard to categorize as a particular type of pattern. They are circular in nature, so we could say they're structural. But they also have to do with how information, feedback information in particular, flows. Causal loops can help us distinguish between complicated and complex dynamics. Complication sees causation in a unidirectional, straight line. Action A directly causes Outcome B. The distance in time and space between A and B is short, observable, and measurable. This is the stuff of classic scientific reasoning. But in complexity, A is rarely close to B in time or space, often unobservable, and seldom does causation flow in one direction. Remember Dr. Lorenz, the meteorologist from Chapter 5 who helped start the science of nonlinear change? He is famous for describing the butterfly effect, the notion that things that happen at a distance can profoundly affect what happens here—wherever here is.

Distal causality happens everywhere, every day. In the story about Marian, the child who was upset that her father was leaving on a business trip, someone, somewhere in corporate America decided someone (Marian's father) needed to be on a plane to Houston Monday morning. That decision impacted an entire class of fourth graders, a fourth-grade teacher, and my morning. In late 2019, a virus that previously only infected wildlife, infected a human in Wuhan China. That illness spread around the world, taking millions of lives and livelihoods. More recently, a hurricane barreling through the south Pacific, hundreds of miles south of the Hawaiian Islands, caused horrific brush fires on Maui that leveled Lahaina, the historic seat of the Hawaiian monarchy, killing over one hundred people and leaving thousands homeless. In complex systems, cause and effect can be separated by vast amounts of space, which means the link between cause and effect is often difficult to detect. Creating models of causal loops (called causal loop diagrams) can help us map how causality, including distal causality, works in systems we're influencing. You can find more information about how to draw and interpret causal loop diagrams on my website.

Change Patterns

Change patterns come about when complex systems shift from relatively steady states to other steady states. For example, a paradigm shift is a special case of collapse (of the existing paradigm) followed by exponential growth (of the new paradigm). In this section, we'll explore four types of change patterns: exponential growth, collapse, threshold effect, and S-curves.

Exponential Growth

Remember, complex systems rarely change in a linear fashion. Back in Chapter 5, we explored how linear change happens and I wrote that when we're trying to affect large-scale change, we don't want linear change. We want disproportional, nonlinear change. That doesn't mean nonlinear change is "good" and linear change is "bad." Nonlinear change is neither good nor bad. It just is. Understanding how it works gives us an edge when working with complex systems.

Exponential growth is a powerful nonlinear change pattern. Prior to 2020, few people were familiar with exponential growth curves. Now, in the wake of the COVID-19 pandemic, we're all too familiar with how exponential growth works. A key characteristic of exponential growth is that it appears to happen out of the blue when in fact the conditions that lead to such drastic change have been smoldering for quite some time. Then wham! They hit what author Malcolm Gladwell wrote about it in his book *The Tipping Point*, and we're living in a whole new world.

Knowing how exponential growth works is key to being an effective changemaker. If we don't understand nonlinear growth, we might look for stair-step, linear change, and if we find none, we believe change efforts aren't working. But when we understand that exponential growth takes a long time to gather steam, rather than giving up, we can take actions that amplify conditions for momentum. Often, when change efforts are funded by government or philanthropy, results, measured by linear methods, are expected long before efforts could ever realize a complex system change.

The converse is also true. It's easy to think a problem isn't a problem because the phenomenon happens so infrequently. Only a *few* kids report bullying. Only *two* garden plants died suddenly. Only a *handful* of angry parents protested the new curriculum. Only a *dozen* people are hospitalized with a new virus. Understanding exponential growth keeps us alert to small changes.

Recognizing exponential growth gives us a head start on taking wise actions to either amplify or dampen conditions that could trigger a tipping point. Imagine a child is having a hard time using multiplication. When an adult poses a multiplication problem or gives the child a worksheet, the child either doesn't respond or responds incorrectly. But the child spontaneously and accurately uses multiplication when building with blocks with other children. We can set conditions to amplify the child's confident use of multiplication by not directly posing questions or giving worksheets, but by providing lots of opportunities to use multiplication in hands-on learning experiences with his peers. It seems simple, but most teachers are unable to deviate from the specified curriculum to use this complexity-based strategy.

In a regenerative school, it would be the norm.

A final word on exponential growth: When we want a phenomenon to take off, say a renewed commitment to caring for Earth, it's easy to do all we can to amplify conditions for increasing growth. I mean, who would even consider dampening renewed commitment to caring for Earth? The more the better, right?

Not so fast.

If we want long-lasting change, we need to set conditions so that systems connected to whatever is rapidly changing have time to reorganize and adapt. That said, often systems reorganize so they can dampen whatever is rapidly changing. If the change happens too fast, systems push back, hard. This is why local, grassroots, flying-under-the-radar approaches to social change are usually far more effective than highly visible, top-down, centralized efforts.

Collapse

Sometimes, exponential change happens in the opposite direction as growth. Collapse is an exponential growth curve flipped upside down. Seemingly without warning, something that seems steady and stable suddenly collapses. Think avalanches, landslides, and the US 2008 housing market. Collapse is a common phenomenon. Like exponential growth, conditions for collapse often go undetected for a long time. Back in June of 2021, with eyes wide and guts clenched, people around the world watched grainy security footage as a Florida condominium complex collapsed in the dead of night, killing dozens. Homeowners knew there were problems with the building, but until that night, life in Champlain Towers South didn't skip a beat. Residents parked cars, greeted neighbors, FaceTimed loved ones, and slept soundly, heedless of the complex forces wearing away the very foundation of their homes.

Because we haven't had our human capacities for recognizing complex patterns nurtured and honed during our formative years, failing to recognize indicators of collapse is all too common. We have an uncanny ability to silence inconvenient warnings. We nudge a toothache to back of mind or ignore the check engine light for one too many miles.

It's no different with education.

Education as we know it is near collapse. Those who recognize collapse as a complex pattern see our educational systems, along with food production and distribution, banking, job markets, housing, and medical systems, among others, as dangerously frail. We don't need to set conditions for education as we know it to collapse. The conditions were set in motion long ago.

Collapse is inevitable.

Threshold Effect

Another critical complex pattern is the threshold effect. We see this pattern when change processes reach natural (or otherwise imposed) limiting conditions. Height is a good example. No one reading this page is twenty feet tall. The tallest trees on Earth are over 370 feet tall, but not 500 feet tall. Height always meets natural threshold effects. When charging batteries, the charge rate slows as the battery nears a full charge. When running a marathon, athletes know they will run more slowly near the end of the race.

Threshold effects run counter to the unlimited growth models of the industrial era. Earth has limited capacity. Just as no athlete, no matter how well trained, can sprint through an entire marathon, Earth has its limits too. Respecting Earth's thresholds is an important part of setting conditions conducive to life and fulfilling our human responsibility to make intelligent contributions to continuing life on Earth.

Keeping threshold effects in mind when trying to influence complex change helps us avoid thinking that an initiative no longer "works" when it hits a plateau that might be nothing more than a naturally occurring threshold effect. When I worked for First Things First in Arizona, there was concern that the growth of a scholarship program had slowed. Enrollment in the program had taken off quickly, but then the numbers of new people applying plateaued. That's a typical complex pattern. The state had a limited number of people wanting and qualifying for the scholarship. The slower uptake when the number of enrolled people hit that plateau did not mean the program was no longer working.

At the individual level, threshold effects are important to understand because children (and adults!) have a limited supply of energy. Rather than seeing wiggles, squirms, and daydreaming as problematic, we can recognize threshold effects and adjust the pace of learning experiences.

The S-Curve

If you couple an exponential growth curve with threshold effects, you get one of the most common complex patterns on the planet: the S-curve. S-curves are so common, an entire approach to creating intelligence and achievement tests, Item Response Theory, is built on them. S-curves are the pattern "under the hood" of most college entrance exams and even assessments of children's development, such as California's Desired Results Developmental Profile (DRDP).

Most learning, most change, and most complex phenomena happen in S-curve patterns. Exponential growth happens when conditions are right for something that's been slowly brewing to hit a tipping point. Then the phenomenon grows like a weed until it hits a naturally occurring (or intentionally imposed) limitation. When it hits the limitation, the growth slows, most often to a plateau, and it stays flat, often while the system is reconfiguring or until it hits growth conditions again that send it into another exponential growth curve. It is very easy to think that when something that has grown at an exponential rate slows down that something is wrong, something isn't working, or, if we're trying to slow growth, that the battle has been won. What's really going on, however, is that complex systems are reorganizing around and adapting to new conditions. That's what keeps happening with COVID-19 variants. The virus keeps adapting and morphing to new conditions, such as increased numbers of people with acquired immunity.

CHAPTER SUMMARY

Key Points

1. Humans are born with innate capacity for developing complex pattern expertise.
2. Expertise is developed not by accumulating knowledge, but by being immersed in complex experiences, even if we do not initially understand those experiences.
3. Learning how to recognize and influence complex patterns is key to setting conditions for a paradigm shift and for creating a whole new regenerative way of doing school.
4. All models are wrong. Some are useful. The complex pattern models offered in the complex pattern primer are wrong, but also useful. The goal isn't precision. The goal is perspective. Hold the models loosely.
5. There are many types of complex patterns. Three critically important kinds of complex patterns are:
   - Structural Patterns, which include swirls and cycles, networks, and fractals.
   - Flow Patterns, which include sinks and checks, and causal loops.
   - Change Patterns, which include exponential growth, collapse, threshold effects, and S-curves.

Playing with Complexity

Individually or with others, use your practice field to explore the So What? phase more deeply. Here are some questions that are especially helpful in the So What? phase:

- So what are the most relevant patterns we've observed? Have we identified patterns in all three categories? Are different aspects of our work affected by different patterns? For example, are adults and children experiencing different patterns?
- So what is changing or moving, and what do those changes mean for what we hope to accomplish?
- So what do the patterns we've observed mean for our work in general, and for our next wise action in particular? Would it be wise to try to influence any of these patterns? If so, how would we want them to shift?

8

How to Influence Complex Systems

A Complex Adaptive System is a cluster of individual parts that interact with each other, and over time systemwide patterns appear. Parts. Interactions. Patterns.
~ Dr. Glenda Eoyang and Royce Holladay

The external cosmic rhythm of the seasons reappears inside living beings, just as we have taken the organization of time, which is that of our calendar and our festivals, from the cosmos to integrate it into our societies. Consequently, the world is in us, just as we are in the world.
~Dr. Edgar Morin

"Could I have a word with you?"

I took a deep breath and joined Camille at the round table where she sat near the front of a large conference room. We had just concluded the morning session with a gathering of early education leaders from twenty-three California counties. Camille was the executive director of First 5 California, the state's early childhood agency. First 5 CA had hired the consulting firm I worked for to design and carry out a nine-million-dollar three-year professional development project for childcare and preschool leaders and teachers. I was hired to direct the project and deeply respected Camille. Heading an education agency in a US state the size of California is daunting, yet she did it with bold leadership and gracious humility.

My team had been charged with creating a two-day in-person learning experience for leaders from participating counties. I had challenged my team to think beyond keynotes and panel discussions. Neither my team nor my supervisor were confident my plan aligned with what Camille wanted, but they supported the direction I wanted to take. The team generated great designs for community building and networking activities, but were stumped about how to create an opening session that would involve the participants as learners rather than the "sit and git" from "experts" that makes up most plenary sessions.

I decided to enlist three colleagues who are whizzes at engaging educators in systems thinking. First, I asked Dr. Peter Senge, author of *The Fifth Discipline* and founder of the Society for Organizational Learning to make a brief video that teed up the day and invited attendees to contemplate why educators need to think in systems. Then, Dr. Tracy Benson and Sheri Marlin of the Waters Foundation, a dynamic duo who give workshops all over the country on systems thinking in education, did a two-hour workshop.

The morning was completely different than most conference plenaries. I had a great time, but did it help anyone shift their thinking? Would our client appreciate what we had tried to do? I was about to find out.

"Ida Rose, this was not at all what I was expecting," Camille said.

My stomach tightened. Oh dear. Systems thinking in education was relatively new, and from the conferences I had attended in California, I knew people expected lofty lectures from the state's plethora of top academics. But I had long before decided to use every opportunity I had to shift people's thinking about what learning is and what education could be. As I listened, I contemplated the possibility that I had moved too fast.

Camille continued, "In my role as executive director, I go to these types of meetings all the time. I welcome people. I say a few words. But at this point in my career I rarely learn anything. That's not what happened today. Today I learned new things I can use in my job, tomorrow. Thank you."

I was delighted that Camille benefitted from the session, but I also knew her response could've been very different. Inviting people into complexity thinking is never a sure thing. Such an invitation asks people to buckle up for what may very well be a bumpy ride. We're asking folks to replace the illusion of control with setting conditions for influence, knowing we cannot control the outcomes. In this chapter, I invite you to tighten your seatbelt. You will encounter some sophisticated concepts that at first may seem too abstract to be practical. But stick with it. I'll give you real-world examples and also help you use the ideas in your own practice field.

A complexity approach to changemaking challenges the notion that we can, or should, predict outcomes. Most of us have so bought into the idea that success is defined by how well we plan and execute, as evidenced by outcomes, that we can't imagine how we can possibly realize desired change when complexity is so capricious.

But we can.

Our most powerful role, as humans, is to act individually and collectively to set conditions that influence complex systems. Setting conditions that influence complexity requires us to shift our thinking from planning, execution, and debrief to recognizing patterns, taking condition-setting actions, and then observing attentively so we can adjust our actions, if necessary.

I can just imagine what you, my dear reader, might be thinking. "What? No measurable outcome? No guarantees?"

Yeah, sorry, no.

Please don't put down the book. You're learning powerful ways to influence societal change. Dancing with complexity requires a ton of patience, trust in the process, and letting go of the need to predict outcomes. We may not have control, but we do have conditions. Knowing how to set them yields enormous changemaking power because complex systems are highly sensitive to conditions.

What Are Conditions and How Do We Set Them?

If complex systems are highly sensitive to conditions, it behooves us to develop deep expertise in conditions and how to set them. Conditions are the states and characteristics of phenomena in an environment. Simple Rules, such as moving fast in a circle and biting the bug before you or thinking passively, are a special, and powerful, kind of condition. An environment consists of anything that affects an individual or system. Sunshine flowing through a window on a cold wintery day is a condition in my environment. So are the reports of wars and political divisiveness I read online this morning.

Conditions foster, maintain, or disrupt complex patterns. When I brush my teeth, I'm disrupting the patterns bacteria are following in my mouth. When I invite people to sit in a circle, I'm setting conditions that foster interaction patterns.

Conditions are also precursors to emergent complex patterns. People set conditions several times each day, every day, but nearly always they do so without awareness or intention. People are accustomed to their actions directly *causing* an outcome, like when we flip on a light switch or step on an accelerator. With those experiences as the status quo, adopting the role of condition-setting agents can seem like trading power for weakness. But setting conditions is the *way* we influence *emergence*. Helping to bring about the emergence of new, complex properties or a whole new complex system is tremendously powerful, more powerful than what we're used to, more powerful than anything industrialism offers us. If we want the patterns we need for whole new ways of doing school to emerge, we need large numbers of people setting conditions for something very different than what we have now.

As educational changemakers, we don't want to set conditions willy-nilly. We want to know what we're doing and to do it intentionally. Every spring, I start seeds for my garden. I don't just throw seeds on dirt. Throwing seeds on dirt does not set conditions conducive to germination. I plant seeds with intentionality. I read about each variety on the seed packet or know from previous experience the needs of the seeds I've saved. Conditions are everything that affects the seeds. Some seeds germinate best when planted in very shallow soil. Others need to be nestled in at a dark depth. Some need to be cold stratified (planted outside in the cold or stored in the fridge for a few weeks). Others like warm soil.

I plant most seeds in light, fluffy, seed-starting mix, mist the soil to keep it damp, and put the seed blocks on a mat that gently warms them. I cover those that like high humidity with a dome. I get great germination rates every year, but, and this is a *major* but, there isn't anything I can do to *make* seeds germinate. Enticing them with an A+ grade or threatening them with failure won't make them germinate. Giving them a good talking to won't do the trick either. All I can do is set conditions conducive to germination. Although I cannot coerce germination, I can *act*. Read back through this paragraph and the one before it and notice all the verbs.

I read.

I plant.

I use.

I cover.

I *act* a lot. And those actions set conditions for complex systems (plants) to emerge. For schools to shift to regenerative learning, we need a cadre of societal changemakers with substantial expertise in setting conditions for regenerative schools to emerge.

How Conditions Influence Complex Systems

Unlike complex systems, complicated systems are not sensitive to conditions. Complicated systems are designed so that they can operate in a wide variety of locations, under all but the most extreme conditions. Your smartphone functions whether you're in Canada or Brazil, scaling a ten-thousand-foot mountain or snoozing at sea level. The phone doesn't care if you're twelve or ninety-two. It doesn't notice your race or gender. It does what it was designed to do regardless of (all but the most extreme) conditions.

Anytime you feel exasperated because you can't resolve a billing issue at a large corporation, you're experiencing the wheels of capitalism turning no matter what you say or do. The system is not sensitive to your needs. Just like a smartphone, the system does what it was designed to do regardless of how much you rant or reason.

Our current schools are similar in that they are designed to function anywhere, except under extreme conditions (such as a remote rural school with only a handful of students). For a decade or so I flew several times each month from the US West Coast to the East. I am a window seat flyer. To pass the time, I played a game whenever we flew above populated areas: find the schools and identify if they are an elementary, middle, high school, or a college. I got very good at picking out schools and identifying their level, mostly by athletic fields and parking lot size. My success isn't surprising. The few companies that build schools in the US have a limited set of plans that get built all over the country.

When I lived in Pennsylvania, I worked at a brand-new elementary school. Several years later, I served a newly built elementary school in Tucson, AZ. The school in Pennsylvania and the school in Arizona were nearly identical. Their structures did not emerge from the unique properties of the surrounding environment, the local culture, or the needs of the children that attended school. Their structures were designed to work anywhere, from the desert of the US Southwest to the mid-Atlantic suburbs. The structures were not sensitive to local conditions.

Not so with complexity. Complex systems are *highly* sensitive to, interact with, and *adapt* to conditions in their environment. The sensitivity of complex systems and their capacity to adapt to immediate environments has many implications for educational change, but a couple are especially important for setting conditions for regenerative schools. First, children, as complex systems, are very sensitive to conditions, even to seemingly insignificant conditions, such as walking in straight lines to go to lunch or being separated by age for twelve years. Therefore, regenerative schools set conditions for young humans to learn and grow as the complex beings they are, rather than as widgets entering the workforce pipeline.

Further, the primary responsibility of teachers in regenerative schools is to set conditions conducive to learning, for each learner and their unique needs, and to create conditions that help learners set their own conditions conducive to learning. In a regenerative school, teachers also teach in ways that set conditions conducive to life, and teach learners to do the same.

Those responsibilities are a huge shift from expecting teachers to deliver a curriculum within an expected timeframe. If we expect teachers to expertly set conditions for learning for all children and prioritize setting conditions conducive to life, society must value them as intellectual and interpersonal heavyweights who are essential to creating a healthy, humane society.

Containers, Differences, and Exchanges

In this section, you'll learn a tool called the CDE framework that can help you develop expertise in setting conditions for complex systems change. CDE stands for *containers*, *differences*, and *exchanges*, and fits hand in glove with Adaptive Action. The CDE framework gives us a practical way to identify opportunities for influencing complex systems.

In Chapter 6 you learned about Adaptive Action, an approach to puzzle-solving in complexity developed by Dr. Glenda Eoyang. Before we get into the CDE model, it is helpful to consider Glenda's definition of complex systems. Glenda uses the term Complex Adaptive Systems (CAS), which she defines as a "cluster of individual parts that interact with each other and over time systemwide patterns appear." In my own writing, I use the generic terms complexity, complex phenomena, and complex system to describe what Glenda calls a CAS.

I share Glenda's definition of a CAS because it offers important clues for understanding conditions and how they can influence complexity. First, a CAS is a "cluster of *individual* parts" (emphasis mine.) Let's contrast that with complicated systems. Complicated systems are made up of *components*, each with a specific purpose. Going back to my oft-used car example, motor vehicles usually have wheels, a way to steer, something that provides locomotion, and components that provide a host of other functions (think a horn or windshield wipers).

Most often, when we think about systems building or change, we think about how we can improve components. Let's revise educational standards, again. Maybe change teacher competencies. Or how about changing the calendar and trying year-round school? This is the stuff of run-of-the-mill reform.

But complex systems are not made up of components. Rather, they are made up of individuals and they form an irreducible whole (think back to Chapters 3 and 4 where I discussed wholeness in depth). It is complex systems' irreducible nature of that makes them hard for us to wrap our heads around. We can't merely pull out one part of the system, fix it, and put it back together. Complex systems are not an amalgam of components. You can go to a junkyard and buy components from a dozen different vehicles and create a new car. But you can't take a hoof from a horse, a tail from a cat, and a head from a cow, cobble them together and get a pig. A pig emerges from a mama pig and will have the identity of a pig for its entire life. Complex systems do everything they can to protect and perpetuate their identity, even if those efforts lead it to become so rigid it cannot adapt.

Our schools are complex systems that are run by complicated, industrial-era rules and are implementing complicated, industrial-era methods. Those methods and purposes are obsolete, and many would argue inhumane. Yet schools and districts are still complex systems. I know that sounds like a contradiction, but it isn't. You know those optical illusions that seem to shape-shift before your eyes from a picture of one thing to another? You've likely seen a picture of an older woman looking forward and down, but if you shift your focus, you'll see a young woman looking away in the same picture. There's another one with two vases, but there's also a face in between. You can find links to several examples on my website if you're unfamiliar with these illusions and would like to check them out.

When we're dealing with a complex social system, such as education, that has adopted complicated ways of functioning, we need to exercise our brain's capacity for shifting between different perspectives, between complicated and complex, to truly understand what's going on. Education as we know it is a complex system using complicated methodologies and perpetuating a complicated purpose and identity. So, it is easy for us to get muddled and think we can fix it with complicated solutions.

But we can't.

Reductionist complicated approaches won't work to "reform" education because they do not address complexity. Science philosopher Dr. Mary Midgley put it this way: "Pure reductionism will not work [for unravelling biological complexity], precisely *because it does not analyze the kind of complexity organisms display*" (emphasis mine).

School Reform efforts can never be anything more than putting lipstick on a pig, because education as we know it cannot change its core identity and purpose.

A gussied-up pig is still a pig.

Real change requires the emergence of something new.

Something new only emerges under the right conditions.

For regenerative schools to emerge, educational changemakers need solid expertise in how complex systems start, work, and change. Because a CAS is comprised of individuals, not components, the system functions differently than complicated systems. Consider tomatoes. If you're thinking that a tomato plant is a complex system because I previously said living systems are complex, you might be confused, because tomato plants have components, right? They have leaves and fruit and stems. Well, yes. But tomato "components" are different in significant ways from car components. Let's think about how a tomato plant comes to be. It emerges when a teensy-tiny seed is planted in conditions conducive to germination. That is very different than how the component parts of a vehicle come into being. Cars come about in a factory that has an assembly line for the engine, another for the body, another for the drivetrain. Then all the components are brought together and assembled.

The car is *built*. Nothing *emerges*.

That isn't how a tomato plant forms, is it? There isn't one seed that builds the leaves and another that manufactures the stems and yet another that produces the roots. Everything the tomato plant needs to be a tomato plant is packed into one tiny seed, and everything that becomes the plant *emerges* from that. Like animals, including people, all of a plant's cells have the same DNA, and those individual cells differentiate into various functions, functions that can change as the plant adapts to its environment. For example, when a tomato cutting is placed in water, the cells that served as a stem change their function and become roots.

This phenomenon of individuals morphing their role from performing one function to another also happens in ant colonies when individual ants change their functions if part of the colony is damaged. So even though complex systems such as tomato plants and ant colonies look like they have components, those components are actually made up of individual cells that can change their roles and adapt their functions, not components that have set, predetermined functions. If a car gets a flat, the radiator doesn't morph into a tire. The radiator and the tire are not made up from the same "cells." The car is comprised of components, not individuals.

So what?

The real power to affect large-scale societal change in any

sector is knowing how to influence the *whole*. Because complex systems are made up of individuals, not components, the key to influencing the *whole* is influencing *individuals*. Our complicated ways of thinking trick us into thinking we've got to identify the component we need to change or influence the entire system all at once.

Elect a different president!

Change the education code!

Create a national curriculum!

But in order to influence the whole, we need to be really good at influencing *individuals*.

Dr. Eoyang has identified three fundamental characteristics of a CAS that can help us identify the individuals in a complex system and better see how to influence them. Those three characteristics are *containers, differences,* and *exchanges*. Containers, differences, and exchanges help us see complex patterns more clearly and provide clues about how we can take condition-setting actions that help us influence individuals. The three characteristics overlap and interact, but to introduce them, let's consider each individually.

Containers refers to that which holds the individuals in a system together. Containers can be physical, such as our bodies, a university campus, a classroom, or a geographical region. They can be ideological, such as religions, philosophies, or political perspectives. Containers can be interpersonal, such as a family, community, or tribal relationships. Shifting containers can affect dramatic and often immediate change.

I've shared several stories about the National Science Foundation project I led in Southeastern San Diego. I learned about the power of containers the hard way while overseeing that project. I implemented the project as I had proposed it, and invited leaders from the community to design a STEM learning ecosystem for young children. I planned an entire weekend, bringing in some of the top US experts in science learning for young children as subject matter resources for the local leaders. The trouble was, only a couple of the leaders invited to the weekend lived in the community. None of them had children in the local schools we were discussing. None of the people in the room were the people who would benefit from or engage with what we were planning. I had not created a container that would be sensitive to local conditions.

At the end of a nearly perfectly executed weekend, using some of the best techniques for gathering community input, I came to terms with the fact that I wasn't working in a useful container. Even with all the intellectual firepower I had gathered, I still didn't have the information I needed to implement something the people in the community wanted and needed. I was faced with the hard truth that I had done what nearly everyone seeking to implement a new educational program does, and if I moved forward with the information I had, I would implement nothing more than a gussied-up pig. It would be another initiative designed by people in power to be implemented with individuals who had little to no say, supposedly for their benefit.

I consulted with my National Science Foundation program officer, told her my concerns, and asked to make major changes to who we engaged and how we engaged them. She granted my request, and I set to work moving the project from the institute I led (it was seen as an elitist organization by many), to the local elementary school that Sylvia Acevedo eventually visited. Changing the container to the neighborhood school allowed me to observe who some of the true community leaders were: the school's office manager, a mom of two young children who was working with a local literacy nonprofit, and the school's principal. I got to know a cadre of moms who deeply wanted to change the way they and their children perceived science and how others perceived their capacity for learning science.

Identifying the important containers helps us by giving us clues to what patterns to anticipate and, if we're skilled, what actions to take in response to those patterns. It helps me "see" containers in the social world if I first think of examples in the physical world. If we were sailing, the boat is a (complicated) container maneuvering in the complex container we call the sea. In the sea, we expect wave and wind patterns. We also watch how the sail interacts with the wind. Is it tight? Is it luffing? A skilled sailor knows how to adjust the sail, a condition-setting action that will influence how the boat moves in the sea. When we anticipate patterns, we can better plan what condition-setting actions to take.

Sitting in the school's office on several mornings allowed me to observe patterns that I hadn't seen from my office several miles away. One of the most important patterns I saw was that adults spoke Spanish far more often than English. One of the changes I made to the project was not to conduct parent focus groups in English with Spanish translation, as I had planned. Instead, I hired the Spanish-speaking mom who worked part-time with the local literacy nonprofit as a coordinator and held the focus groups in Spanish with English translation for me and a research associate. I started each focus group by acknowledging that even though I was born and raised in San Diego, I did not speak Spanish, and I apologized that I had not honored their language by learning to speak it despite living where it was spoken for most of my life. I acknowledged them as the experts on their children and what their children's futures. I also made sure parents were involved in decision-making.

By changing venues and my approach, I broadened the container so that people who would not otherwise have participated were not only welcomed but had decision-making power. Broadening a container is not a gimmick. We don't do it to gain engagement and continue on with top-down, hierarchical practices. Reverence, reciprocity, and mutual thriving hold no space for manipulating people. Rather, equity, *real* equity, emerges when these values are fully embraced. Containers that hold reverence, reciprocity, and mutual thriving for everyone are the only containers that can facilitate the kind of interactions that set conditions for the emergence of regenerative schools.

Before we consider differences, I want us to remember that Earth is a universally important container. The conditions needed for Earth to thrive are the same conditions humans need. Understanding the relationship of humans and Earth is fundamental to setting conditions for a regenerative society and the kind of schools that will perpetuate it. In 2000, the United Nations Educational, Scientific, and Cultural Organization (UNESCO) commissioned French philosopher Dr. Edgar Morin to write a white paper on education. He focused primarily on the need to shift education from a reductionist, machine paradigm to complex approaches to learning, but also emphasized the need to understand Earth as a whole: "In this planetary era we have to situate everything in the planetary complex and context. Learning about *the world as world* has become a vital and intellectual necessity" (emphasis mine).

Schools that hold the regenerative values of reverence, reciprocity, and mutual thriving will embrace setting conditions conducive to life as their central priority. Unlike education as we know it, where schools emerge from the profit priorities of industrialism, in regenerative schools every decision and every investment of resources revolve around the conditions needed for Earth, and all that Earth holds, to thrive.

Differences refers to ways one or more things are not the same. Complexity is generated by difference. As I described in Chapter 3, depth perception is a complex phenomenon generated by the differences between the two images our eyes create. In Chapter 2, Aisha at the zoo adapted her animal concepts when she encountered her family members' different reaction to her calling an elephant a dog. Calling an animal "doggy" had always worked before. Now it didn't. Something was different. Aisha's uncle set conditions for disrupting Aisha's mental model by amplifying the differences between the two animals. If we shift our mental model of learning from an accumulation of knowledge to adaptation to the environment and the emergence of something new, then it follows that *differences are necessary for learning*. Yet education as we know it forces similarities every day.

All children attend school the same number of hours and days.

All children learn the same curriculum.

All children are expected to meet the same standards.

As I write this, a young man in Texas is serving the second suspension of his senior year because the dress code of the public school he attends mandates short hair. He refuses to reject part of his cultural identity merely because his school demands uniformity. Welcoming diversity is not just about being nice to people who differ from the majority in some way. I want schools to respect all people, of course, but I also want students with a wide range of skin tones, cultural backgrounds, hairstyles, and languages all interacting and learning together because diverse communities is a condition conducive to life. Monocultures choke ecosystems, including human learning ecosystems. Forced similarities are dangerous because they extinguish individuals' novel characteristics that benefit everyone.

As important and well-intentioned as Diversity, Equity, and Inclusivity efforts are in education, they are pushing futilely against a fundamental problem: industrial schools prize similarity and distain diversity. Education as we know it tramples our natural embrace of human diversity and turns it into something so foreign that we need special programs to convince us to value all people. Devaluing diversity is dangerous in all areas of life, but sometimes it's hard to see just how destructive it can be.

As I immerse myself more and more into learning about our food systems, I learned about a sad connection between where I grew up and my ancestral homeland that helped me understand how fundamentally important diversity is to all complex living systems. I grew up ninety minutes south of Disneyland, located in Orange County, California. When I was a child, I remember driving there through acres and acres of orange groves, the sea of deep green leaves dotted with ripening fruit, stretching in all directions. Drive in Orange County today and you'll be lucky to see a few orange trees peeking over backyard walls. A legend on my father's side has it that Walt Disney purchased one of the groves he needed to build Disneyland from my stepmother's uncle, so I had felt a special kinship with the oranges that grew there from my early years. Then I learned how those crops economically devastated Sicily, my maternal ancestral homeland.

In his book *Eating to Extinction*, BBC food journalist Dan Saladino (also a person of Sicilian descent) tells the story of how oranges, specifically navel oranges, wound up in Southern California and how, currently, all fresh citrus is endangered because of the monoculture methods used to grow them. In gripping prose, Dan tells the economic, political, cultural, and agricultural tale of how monoculture orange production not only led to the collapse of citrus orchards and the villages they supported in Sicily, but massive infestations of Asian citrus psyllid and the incurable disease they have spread in Florida and California.

Valuing mutual thriving prompts us to care about the economic devastation to Sicilian towns, but losing Sicily's oranges has effects beyond the island with implications for the well-being of all humanity. Dr. David Sinclair, a Harvard geneticist who studies the causes of age-related diseases, such as cancer, heart disease, and Alzheimer's, is famous for identifying a compound in red fruits and vegetables called resveratrol. Resveratrol acts as an anticancer, antioxidant, antiaging, and anti-inflammatory agent. The research on resveratrol is still evolving, but, for example, in 2019, researchers at University of Catania on the island of Sicily found that the juice of blood oranges reversed liver disease in laboratory animals, while the juice of blond (non-red) oranges grown in the same area did not. Conversely, some studies of resveratrol in isolation found little evidence that it prevents serious disease. Why the confusing findings?

Diseases are complex and are therefore caused—and prevented—by a multitude of chemical and genetic interactions. One such interaction is between resveratrol and molecules called anthocyanin. Anthocyanins are the compounds that give purple fruits and vegetables their color. If you're lucky enough to find one, when you eat a blood orange, you're eating both resveratrol *and* anthocyanin. The secret sauce appears to be the presence and interactions of *different* compounds in the *whole* fruit. Blood oranges, with their beneficial combination of resveratrol and anthocyanins, are smaller and not as juicy as navel oranges. They were driven to the edge of extinction because they are not a profitable commodity.

Monoculture doesn't just threaten agriculture. Human diversity is a critical form of biodiversity, and yet, as with the young man in Texas whose senior year was derailed by a dress code, schools everywhere treat diversity as problematic. When I was a doctoral candidate at the University of Arizona, I observed first-year teachers as a research assistant on a federally funded project. One day, I observed a first-year second-grade teacher conducting a lesson on cowboys during rodeo week. Tucson, where the University of Arizona is located, has a rich ranch history. The annual rodeo is such a big deal that schools close for a two-day holiday every February.

The teacher, a middle-age white woman, sat on a chair with her students, all Latino-appearing children in a school whose population was over 98 percent Latino, seated around her on a rug. One by one she held up flashcards, each with a picture of something associated with ranching, and asked what it was. One card had a picture of the heavy pants ranch hands wear. A boy seated near the front shot his hand in the air. I could see the corners of his mouth turned up in a big grin as he sat up straight, hand held high.

The teacher called on him.

"*Pantalones*!" he exclaimed.

"No," the teacher said, shaking her head, and pointed to another student.

The boy slouched, rested his chin on closed fists, and stared at the floor. He remained that way for the rest of the lesson, not even glancing at the other cards. I looked up at a nearby bulletin board decorated with a dozen pictures of cowboys, all white men. How different this classroom was from Pūnana Leo O Maui.

Nowhere in this classroom or lesson were there representations of the rich heritage of Mexican or Native American rancheros. Nowhere were the *vaqueros*, the skilled herdsmen of the US Southwest, mentioned. The teacher's response to the boy's use of his heritage language easily communicated that it, and the culture from which it emerged, were not welcome at school.

After the lesson the children went to lunch, and I met with the teacher to conduct the research interview. We sat at her desk next to shelving covered with NASCAR memorabilia, model cars, small team flags, and pictures of her and her family with NASCAR drivers. The teacher gestured toward the shelves and said, "I call this my NASCAR shrine. I set it up every year so my students can get to know me and what's important to me."

I finished the interview, gathered my belongings, went out to my car, and wept. I wept for the children who were being taught daily in hundreds of small and unnamed ways that the core of their identity wasn't welcome at their school. I also wept for the teacher who seemed oblivious to the harm she caused, and for the educational system that normalized treating young humans with such irreverence.

I also wept because education as we know it is designed to perpetuate human monoculture. Earth is filled with immeasurable diversity for a reason. This fostering of human monoculture is one of the most corrosive aspects of industrial schools. Celebrating human differences is core to fulfilling our responsibility as stewards and protectors of life on Earth.

Exchanges refers to giving and receiving. Exchanges happen throughout our complex world at all scales from microscopic to the farthest reaches of the universe. To many complexity scientists, exchanges are what define complex systems. Astrophysicist Dr. Erich Jantsch in his book *The Self-Organizing Universe*, put it this way: "An organism is not defined by the sum of the properties of its cells.... A system becomes observable and definable as a system through its interactions."

Exchanges can be between similar individuals, such as between people or animals of the same species, or they can be between dissimilar things, such as when animals and plants exchange oxygen and carbon dioxide with the atmosphere. Reciprocity is a special and important type of exchange. Reciprocity does not imply exchange of equal value. Reciprocity refers to exchanges that provide mutual benefit.

In the foreword to Joanna Macy's book *A Wild Love for the World*, David Abram describes his experience hearing a recording of Macy as he was driving through New York City. "I had been taught about respiration and photosynthesis as two entirely separate, basically mechanical processes. Somehow, I had never noticed how mutually entangled these two activities are.... I had surely never thought of plants as breathing.... Plants just 'give off' oxygen automatically, don't they? Yet the more I thought about it, the more I saw the perfectly analogous nature of these two processes, one zoological and one botanical.... *the mechanical jargon of college biology had blocked me from noticing the utter wonder of the thing*: What the plants are breathing out, all us animals are breathing in. And what we animals are breathing out, all the plants are breathing in. The exquisite reciprocity remains astonishing to me even today—a magic pulse of interspecies generosity..." (emphasis mine).

Exchanges also contribute to many of the complex patterns we explored in Chapter 7. Flow patterns, for example, nearly always involve exchanges. For example, conversations are exchanges where thoughts, perspectives, and information flows. When we buy a sandwich at a local café, the ingredients for our lunch flowed through many exchanges, such as bakers exchanging money for flour and meat producers exchanging money for turkey, before the ingredients are assembled by a person who exchanges their time and skill for monetary compensation, and then places the assembled sandwich in a basket for which we exchange money.

Thinking about how flows behave can help us identify where we can act to influence a system. We can consider:

- *how* resources and information flow,
- *who* has access to those flows, and
- *what* is required in exchange (do I need to chop off my braids?).

Exchanges also create structural patterns. Networks emerge from and are maintained by exchanges between individuals or organizations.

Exchanges have particular relevance for education. Education is, at its core, exchanges among learners (some of whom we call teachers). The quality and nature of exchanges is a core consideration when creating regenerative schools. What is exchanged for what, and by whom? Who gets to know what? Who gets to decide? To what degree are the exchanges in the network based on reciprocity? On coercion? What actions will be taken, both in the design and implementation phases, to set conditions so that exchanges reflect a commitment to reverence, reciprocity, and mutual thriving?

Using CDE to Influence Complex Patterns

The CDE (containers, difference, and exchanges) framework is a useful way to identify opportunities for condition-setting actions. Let's revisit the story about Marian, the fourth-grader from Chapter 7 who was upset about her father leaving on a business trip, to see how an understanding of complex patterns coupled with the CDE framework helped me set conditions that influenced the situation.

First, and perhaps most importantly, I intentionally didn't try to get Marian to stop crying. Her brain was flooded with survival chemicals that produce what we experience as anxiety. When human brains are busy surviving, the chemicals in our bodies that produce "emergency" emotions surge into our bloodstream in an exponential growth pattern. Those emergency emotions subside only when the perception of threat eases. An adult insisting that Marian stop crying would only heighten her anxiety as now her out-of-control-emotions would be displeasing a grownup.

Once triggers are no longer present, a threshold effect kicks in somewhere between ten and twenty minutes. Knowing this, I acted to set conditions that would allow Marian's emotions to run their course, hit a threshold, and collapse. I created a safe container, my office, to let her body and mind work through her emotions, and to cut off exchanges with her classmates and teacher that could trigger another influx of the emergency chemicals. I also acted to create a safe container by requesting consent ("Your teacher asked me to talk with you, is that okay?"). Emergency emotions can be triggered, and their effects exacerbated, when we feel powerless. We rarely revere children by asking their consent, and yet doing so is a primary way we model reverence. No one asked Marian's consent for her father to leave, and she likely had no choice but to attend school even though she was upset.

As she began to regulate her anxiety, I asked Marian questions that helped her shift her emotional container from the classroom, where she had been distressed, to her family, setting conditions for her to feel emotionally connected to trusted caregivers. Then I introduced an activity that helped her shift the mental exchanges she was having about her father's absence by pairing thoughts about her dad with enjoyment (things she liked to do with Dad) rather than fear ("What if his plane crashes?"). The activity also helped her maintain her anticipation of enjoyment (the paper chain).

By asking her to go to the restroom, I set conditions for her to experience those feelings of enjoyment in a different container (the restroom) before heading back to the container where she had been so distraught. A quick trip to the restroom also set conditions for her to experience feeling safe even though she was alone, empowering her to realize she was personally capable of handling the situation.

To be clear, I did not follow a recipe, nor did I have a psychology textbook on my desk opened to a chapter on helping distraught fourth graders. As the exchanges unfolded, if you would have asked me what I was doing, I probably could not have told you. I was in the flow of expertise, expertise heavily influenced by complexity thinking. The more you think in complexity, the more you will act effectively to influence it, and the more you will see how your actions set conditions and how those conditions create change.

As regenerative educational changemakers, it's critical to develop expertise in setting conditions on the fly, in the moment. Establishing regenerative learning nodes here, there, and everywhere is how we set conditions for large-scale societal change. But getting those regenerative learning nodes established will take large numbers of individuals interacting with each other in noncompetitive, reverent ways that foster mutual thriving. The CDE model gives us an effective starting point for shifting from coercing others or using top-down hierarchical power to setting conditions for mutual understanding and respect.

CHAPTER SUMMARY

Key Points

1. We influence complex systems by setting conditions because complex systems are highly sensitive to conditions. Complicated systems are not.
2. Our most powerful role as humans is to act individually and collectively to set conditions that influence complex systems.
3. Conditions are the states and characteristics of phenomena in an environment. Simple Rules are a special, and powerful, kind of condition. They foster, maintain, or disrupt complex patterns.
4. Because children are complex systems that are highly sensitive to conditions, in regenerative schools, experiences are designed to set conditions for young humans to learn and grow as the complex beings they are, rather than widgets entering the workforce pipeline.
5. CDE stands for containers, differences, and exchanges. The framework fits hand in glove with Adaptive Action and gives us a practical way to identify opportunities for influencing complex systems.
   - *Containers* refers to that which holds the individuals in a system together.
   - *Differences* refers to ways one or more things are not the same.
   - *Exchanges* refers to giving and receiving. Reciprocity is a special and important type of exchange. Reciprocity does not imply exchange of equal value. Reciprocity refers to exchanges that provide mutual benefit.

Playing with Complexity

For this Playing with Complexity exercise, we're going to take things a bit out of order. I'd like you to go back to the What? phase and, after reviewing the description you generated in Chapter 6, I'd like you to identify what containers, differences, and/or exchanges are relevant and important to your playing field. Containers might include ideologies that are holding together the people who want the project to move forward. They might include the community or neighborhood that your regenerative school will serve (keeping in mind your regenerative school might be a scout group meeting in your backyard). Containers might also include your own sense of urgency or the motivation of the group of people invested in your efforts.

Do the same for differences and exchanges. What differences are relevant and important? Are there differences in ideologies or motivations among your team? Are there differences between your team and the community you hope to engage? What patterns of exchanges are relevant and important? As you do this exercise, prompt yourself (and others if working together) to think in patterns. Also think about how CDE dynamics overlap: what exchanges do different containers hold? How might containers keep important differences from interacting with each other?

Now move on to the So What? phase and explore the meaning, the So What? of the CDEs you identified in the What? phase. For example, so what does it mean that your group is comprised of people who hold different ideologies about education or politics? So what does it mean if your group has different motivations than many others in the community you hope to engage? So what networks might the exchanges you've identified form? How might those networks improve or impede your efforts?

Write a brief summary of each of these exercises. If you're working in a group, it's helpful for everyone to write their own summary and then for the group to come together to create a collective summary. That said, please do not spend time wordsmithing the summary. It is just a tool. It's okay if it's messy.

9

Designing Regenerative Schools

Design is the conscious process of making culture.
~ Peter Bane

Never doubt that a small group of thoughtful,
committed citizens can change the world;
indeed, it's the only thing that ever has.
~ Dr. Margaret Mead, anthropologist

Living in a way that regenerates Earth can only be realized on a societal scale by society embracing a completely different way of thinking.

Our global problems emerged from our current ways of thinking. Our current ways of thinking cannot fix them.

I hope that when enough people develop expertise in complexity thinking and commit to the Regenerative Values of reverence, reciprocity, and mutual thriving, society's paradigm will shift from an extractive to a regenerative worldview. I hope by now I've made a solid enough case for the need to start with schools.

As critical as they are to a flourishing future, regenerative schools won't magically appear. They will only come about with focused intentionality. I'm eager to share ideas about how to make that happen, but I want to reiterate that I'm not necessarily talking about a place where children go to be taught by adult teachers. Though you can use the ideas in this book to design such a school, remember that I use the term "schools" to mean *any* place or time intentionally set aside for learning of *any* kind and for *any* age and collection of people. Regenerative schools are rooted in reverence, reciprocity, and mutual thriving. It doesn't matter what curriculum, if any, a school uses, if the core values are regenerative, if the school prioritizes setting conditions conducive to life and following Rules for Regeneration, it's a regenerative school.

Don't worry if you don't have the means or desire to start a school (as society currently defines them). That's not a problem. In fact, it's a good thing, because to bring about a whole new way of doing school we need dozens and hundreds of small efforts cropping up everywhere, all networked by a common commitment to Regenerative Values and ways of teaching and learning based on the Simple Rules for Regeneration. I encourage you to think about what *you*, personally, can do. I can't emphasize enough that large-scale social change is most likely to happen when small individual efforts that are initially disconnected from each other emerge, grow, and then connect.

No effort is too small.

A scout troop focused on sustainable living skills and grounded in Regenerative Values isn't too small. A regenerative community garden with folks helping each other learn how to grow food locally isn't too small.

Importantly, no matter the size of your efforts, I encourage you to avoid typical "strategic planning" processes. They are nearly all based on linear and dichotomous thinking. It makes no sense to use approaches based on the Rules of the Drill to create regenerative schools. For example, please don't do a SWOT (strengths, weaknesses, opportunities, threats) analysis. Using these categories is a classic complicated approach that will create more complication. From a complexity science perspective, all strengths are weaknesses and vice versa. All threats are opportunities, and vice versa. The CDE framework, embedded in Adaptive Action cycles, is fit for complex work. SWOT analysis (and approaches like it) is not. Also, please avoid sage on the stage panel discussions. Instead, harvest the wealth of wisdom present in the pews.

Regenerative schools that emerge from the unique conditions in their local niche will be resilient, relevant, and effective. They will influence myriad individuals that make up the whole of society. Their strength and power come from their inherent diversity and inclusivity, emerging from local culture and assets, being small enough to be nimble, and embracing reverence, reciprocity, and mutual thriving. The term regenerative is gaining traction as a way to think about humans' relationship with Earth. It has been most frequently used to describe agricultural practices that regenerate soil and ecosystems. Regenerative agriculture is similar to permaculture practices, which have been used globally for decades, and wilding practices, used especially by Indigenous peoples for millennia. The idea that the principles behind regenerative ways of growing food could be applied to how we live as a society and raise our young is new thinking, at least for anyone not from an Indigenous community.

To give you an example that you can use alongside your own practice field, let's imagine we're living in a small city, and a group of us want to create a community center that will house an afterschool learning resource center, an intergenerational demonstration garden and seed library, a homeschool co-op, and a makerspace with an equipment and tool lending collection along with workshops and classes. We decide to meet weekly at a local library to plan. I'll use this example as a practice field throughout the rest of this chapter. Let's start by exploring what design is and how we can use design concepts in our work.

Design Considerations

Design is tangible imagination. It is a plan, but so much more. We can design physical things such as buildings, clothing, or heart stents. But we can also design social programs, events, and research studies.

Design is a *complicated* process. So why a chapter on a complicated process, when what we need are schools grounded in complexity?

Because when it comes to design, complication is all we've got.

You read that right.

You have come to the gut-level reason why I have painstakingly differentiated complication and complexity. Developing the capacity to differentiate these two dynamics *and* to see both simultaneously, is critical to designing regenerative schools. Way back in the early chapters, I said that we would eventually talk about how complexity and complication work together, but that we needed to first tease them apart so we could get a better idea what each of them are and how they operate. Well, here we are, ready to learn how to use both.

The frameworks and processes in this chapter are intended to prompt you to stay in the mix of complication and complexity, of design and regeneration, rather than slipping into designing reductionist schools unawares. You will likely find yourself creating complicated rules, rubrics, or checklists. That's okay. When you recognize that you've slipped into complication, take a break, and shift back to complex ways of thinking.

Design is the intentional arrangement of elements, relationships, and patterns. *Collections* of *actions* and *elements* thoughtfully selected and arranged are powerful. When I plant my spring crops, I don't just plant in healthy soil. I also choose my timing carefully; provide the sown seeds with warmth, light, and protection; and water them appropriately. See? A *collection* of actions. When I worked with Marian, the distraught fourth grader, I did the same thing. I invite you to go back to Chapter 7 and read that story again, listing the actions I took.

Why am I spending so much time emphasizing action? Because actions are powerful. We can dream, aspire, hope, wish, imagine, and desire. None of it affects change unless we act. Often, we act sequentially, trying, for the sake of efficiency, to see which *one* action works. However, influencing complex systems almost always requires a collection of actions.

This is where *design considerations* come into play. They are what the term implies: *considerations*. Design considerations are things we contemplate and play with, either in our minds or in our dialogue, or, most helpfully, in a sketch (I like to call them scribbles) that help us choose options that, working together, become more than the sum of their parts. The first eight chapters of this book introduced ideas and frameworks that can serve as design considerations for regenerative schools: Rules for Regeneration, Regenerative Values, Complex Patterns, and CDE. Regenerative design processes are not like a cookbook where you choose the end result, gather ingredients, and follow directions to get a predetermined outcome. Rather, in regenerative design we keep multiple perspectives in mind and shift our thinking and perspective to see how complication and complexity interact while the design emerges. Adaptive Action can help us work effectively with complexity and keep us from slipping into complication. Let's go through the frameworks and ideas we've already discussed and see how they can be used as design considerations.

Regenerative Rules Design Considerations

Regenerative Rules are complex Simple Rules, not must-dos or do-nots. Simple Rules generate self-organizing behavior among individuals in complex systems, which is the precursor to emergent (whole new) properties. Simple Rules happen all around us all the time and lead to all kinds of emergent properties, some we want, others we don't. Remember, as you're reading this, microbes in your mouth are following Simple Rules that allow them to proliferate and decompose your teeth.

Quick! Go floss!

Although we live by Simple Rules every day, we are often unaware of the rules we're following and what emerges (or is prevented from emerging) from following those rules. To create schools that teach Regenerative Values, the people designing them must set and intentionally follow Simple Rules. I cannot say this emphatically enough: Don't even consider starting a regenerative school design process without first ensuring everyone involved understands what Simple Rules are and how they work, and without collectively agreeing upon what Simple Rules you will follow. Deciding how you will come to agreement (or disagreement) is one of the most fundamental and powerful rules you can decide.

Simple Rules apply to *how* you design and *what* you design. Frequently review your Simple Rules. Also ask how your Simple Rules will show up in your school. The Regenerative Rules I've suggested are a good place to start, but don't hesitate to modify them. I've listed them here for convenience, with a reminder of what they mean and how they can be applied to designing regenerative schools.

Think in Wholes

When you start a design process, identify what the wholes are. When designing a school, the learners are wholes, and the community the school will serve is a whole. These wholes are nested in other wholes (see Think in Networks, below), and each whole is comprised of individuals. In our imaginary practice field, we ask ourselves who the individuals are that make up the wholes we're designing the community center for. Is it the entire city? A specific community or neighborhood? Is the city's homeschooling community an important whole? Is the community of people whose children attend traditional schools an important whole? Thinking in wholes reminds us to consider boundaries (which we'll also consider when we think about containers). Who and what are in and who and what are out? When I was leading efforts to create a professional development system for the state of Arizona, one of the most difficult considerations was the boundary. Were we designing for *everyone* who cared for and educated young children? Or were we designing for credentialed professionals only, who make up only a small percent of early childhood caregivers and teachers?

Think in Circles

Thinking in circles keeps us mindful of flows, feedback loops, and cycles. How will we use circular thinking in our design process? How will our planning group gather feedback about what we have in mind for the community center? In what ways will we incorporate natural cycles such as the seasons or lunar phases in our design process and in the school itself?

Think Dynamically

Nearly every strategic planning process I've been involved in has operated under the simple rule: Design Something Static. No one ever said, "Let's design something that doesn't change." But, again, Simple Rules usually operate outside our awareness. When you think dynamically, you intentionally design for *change that changes*, and because change changes, it is unpredictable. Schools need routines and structure. But in a regenerative school, everyone is aware that change is expected, and that change is expected to change. In our community center planning sessions, we discuss how we will ensure we can adapt to unforeseen changes. We agree we want Simple Rules that prevent current decisions (such as location, who the school will serve, even the school's purpose) from being carved in stone. We decide that one of our Simple Rules will be *Review and reconsider all policies and decisions at least annually*. We also want to be able to respond nimbly and effectively to unexpected change. Unfortunately, "quickly" is a synonym for nimbly, yet one of the most effective responses to unexpected change is to pause and slow down.

My first education job, when I was a mere eighteen years old, was driving a school bus for San Diego Unified School District. Yes, they not only allowed teenagers to drive buses but they recruited us. We went through extensive training and, if I do say so myself, I was a damn good bus driver, but still! Eighteen! Part of our training, which was conducted by the California Highway

Patrol, was about avoiding crashes, especially on a crowded freeway. Here's the simple rule they taught us: When traffic gets crowded or something unexpected happens up ahead (such as debris on the road or someone driving erratically) *slow down* and create a cushion of space around your bus. It always amazes me how many people don't follow this simple rule. It seems so obvious! But let's consider why it is important. It isn't necessarily that a heavy vehicle needs a lot of time to completely stop. The most important reason is that reduced speed and a cushion of space gives the driver more time to react safely.

Dynamic change can be perilous because it can easily trigger knee-jerk reactions that ignite even more dynamic change, and there isn't enough wiggle room in how the system is acting to give us time to respond rather than react. Using Adaptive Action helps us slow down when faced with dynamic situations. Yes, emergencies demand immediate action. But often dynamic change masquerades as something urgent when it's wise to take our time. What Simple Rules can we adopt to ensure we respond to dynamic change effectively?

Think in Networks

Identifying linkages that need to be cultivated with individuals or organizations is key to building a supportive network. What is connected to what? Who is connected to whom? At our first planning meeting, we start to map resource flows, and discuss how to build connections to asset sources. We are fortunate to have donated space, but recognize we need expertise, influence, lifeways, and knowledges we don't yet have on our team. We decide that developing networks will be part of every planning discussion.

Think Generatively

During my service on the Human Systems Dynamics Institute (HSDI) board, I learned what it means to be a "generative board." Yes, we approve minutes and review budgets, but the primary purpose of the board is *generativity*. To generate ideas and questions, new directions and connections. I've served on six nonprofit boards. Before HSDI, I had never heard the term "generative board" or experienced how Simple Rules can promote generatively.

Learning to be generative as the default takes collective intentionality. Generativity is the core of regeneration, not just linguistically, but conceptually. Regeneration is ensuring our actions set conditions that not only protect and conserve resources but generate enough yield for mutual thriving. Generativity is distinctly different from *productivity*. Productivity has to do with *product* and *profit*. It is focused on controlling work to increase product output. Generativity is about setting conditions for self-organizing that leads to emergence (of something entirely new).

As we begin to plan the community center, we agree to remind ourselves what we want to generate. We ask ourselves what we need to do to set conditions for the yields we want and how our school will support learners as generative beings. We consider what it will take for the entire school to be generative, and decide that we will explicitly engage people around the idea of generativity and help them differentiate it from productivity.

Regenerative Values as Design Considerations

Regenerative Values distinguish regenerative schools from education as we know it. Like Rules for Regeneration, don't start a design process before first making sure everyone involved understands and agrees on the values that will shape both *how* you design and *what* you design. Also, like Rules for Regeneration, the Regenerative Values I've identified are not written in stone. You might need to add to them or revise them for your particular needs. However, please think carefully before eliminating any of them. The three I've suggested are inextricably connected and fundamental to regenerative learning. Reverence moves us to reciprocity and caring about mutual thriving. Mutual thriving requires reciprocity. And reciprocity moves us to reverence as we realize how connected we are.

Our community center planning team agrees to adopt the three Regenerative Values recommended here. We discuss what actions we will take to ensure our values show up, not merely as words, but in actual practice, both in our design process and in the school we're designing. For example, we devote a meeting to discuss how mutual thriving will be prioritized for all the learners. We set aside another meeting to consider how reverence will be evident in everyday interactions between learners, especially when there might be a power differential such as between adults and children or youth. We spend the next meeting deciding what forms of reciprocity will be expected and ensuring our commitment to reverence and mutual thriving influence those decisions.

Complex Patterns as Design Considerations

In Chapter 7, we explored structural, flow, and change patterns. Each person in the community center planning group chooses to become an expert in a type of complex pattern and to act as internal consultant to the design team. From those efforts, our group learns that exchanges between individuals is one of the primary ways networks form, and that multiple exchanges where everyone benefits (reciprocity and mutual thriving) strengthens network connections. During one meeting, we consider how the community center can create opportunities for exchanges that foster mutual benefit. Could we host workshops where expert welders, tech folks, or food preservation specialists work alongside people who are learning these skills? We ask ourselves what other regenerative learning nodes we might want to network with and how those connections might foster mutual benefit.

We decide to commit to a couple discussions to consider cycles and how energy and resources flow in patterns that create feedback loops. We spend time contemplating how we will help learners explore cycles and circular patterns, and identify the feedback loops that we want to set conditions for. We intentionally decide that we want to normalize giving and receiving feedback and adapting to it.

We also consider how change patterns informs our design. We ask what in the environment, immediate and extended, is growing exponentially? What is on the brink of collapse? We note that political divisiveness is increasing exponentially in our small city, threatening community cohesiveness. We agree that meticulously and regularly focusing on Regenerative Values is key to dampening divisiveness and amplifying community cohesiveness, so we decide to make our values highly visible on signage and documents, and to talk about them often and with intentionality.

CDE as Design Considerations

Finally, let's consider CDE. The first Regenerative Rule, Think in Wholes, prompts us to consider which containers we're working with or trying to influence, how differences show up in our planning, which exchanges are already happening, and which exchanges need to happen. Some of the containers you need to consider, however, might be components of complicated systems. You will likely need to consider laws or regulations at the local, state or provincial, and perhaps at the national or federal level. Perhaps you need to consider interactions with a subcommittee on a local governing board of a nonprofit or a city council or school board.

Our community center planning team identifies the local Chamber of Commerce as an important container to engage, as well as an urban agriculture organization, the local school district, and a homeschool collaborative. We also recognize that there are ideological containers that cross the boundaries of organizational containers. For example, there have been tensions between parents whose children attend the local public schools, those who choose to have their children attend a private religious school in the town down the highway, those who homeschool their children, and others who have enrolled their children in a hybrid (remote and in-person) charter school. As complexity thinkers, our planning group recognizes that these different educational containers often represent differences in ideological approaches to education. Rather than excluding anyone based on ideology or ignoring the tensions these differences hold, we recognize tension as a necessary dynamic of complex systems that can lead to robust and innovative generativity. Early in our planning process, we host a community meeting, intentionally inviting families who participate in all schooling choices. In doing so, we create a new container, one that can effectively and reverently contain differing ideologies and approaches to education in the same space. The new container sets conditions for new exchanges between people and invites them into a generative process where they can collectively contribute to creating a new community learning venue.

Putting It All Together

Done well, design gives us much to consider. It helps to have a conceptual container to hold it all and to connect considerations in useful ways. In this section, we'll use Adaptive Action as a design process. As a brief review, Adaptive Action includes three phases:

What?—Create a useful definition and description of the situation. What are you dealing with? A new regenerative high school where adolescents direct their course of study? A sustainable living community center? What is the purpose of the project? What obstacles will you encounter? What are your values and priorities? Identify relevant and important patterns.

So What?—Explore why the What? matters. So what about this project is important? So what effect do we want it to have in our community? So what do the patterns that we identified in the What? phase mean? What is their relevance?

Now What?—What are the next wise actions? Do we need to finesse more carefully what we're doing? Do we need more specific information?

Each Adaptive Action phase has two fundamental tasks: generativity and closure. In each phase, we generate ideas and insights and then close by deciding what to bring forward into the next phase. Before I walk you through Adaptive Action as a design process, I want to give you a few approaches to fostering generativity because opening and maintaining a generative thinking space is rare in decision-making discussions. We often edit ourselves because we want the "right" answer. Even more rare is effectively closing generative thinking spaces, so I'll give you a few options for closing the space and making decisions.

The first approach to fostering generativity is one of the Simple Rules we follow on the board of the Human Systems Dynamics Institute: stand in inquiry, which means we are intentionally curious and actively seek others' perceptions and opinions. Inquiry requires that we ask *generative* questions. At a basic level, generative questions are open-ended, not closed. They are questions that cannot be answered with one word. They are not the kinds of questions a worried parent asks a teenager who just got home an hour past curfew:

Parent: "Where were you?"
Teenager: "Out."
Parent: "Do you know what time it is?"
Teenager: "Late."

Generative questions do not imply judgement, nor are they veiled attempts to advocate a solution. For example:

- "Have you considered that your employment problems are related to your alcohol consumption?"
- "Wouldn't we be able to move forward more quickly if we didn't include people whom we disagree with?"
- "Would there be a larger teacher applicant pool if we adopted a standard curriculum?"

Generative questions nudge open windows of novel thoughts and ideas. For example:

- "What is most important to us in this project?"
- "What do we hope to see come from our efforts?"
- "What are our greatest fears?"
- "Who needs to be involved that is not yet involved?"

I often use a powerful generative activity that originated with HSDI. It's called the Power of Questions. It can be done at any time, takes about twenty minutes, costs nothing, and works in person or online. First, someone volunteers to moderate the experience. The moderator serves as timekeeper, but also reminds folks to only ask generative questions (we all need reminders). If people have gathered with the specific intent to engage in the Power of Questions (some groups do this activity daily or once each week), then someone has usually signed up in advance to pose a question. However, the Power of Questions can also be used on the fly. Once a group of people have learned how to do it, anyone can say, "I'd like to take a break for a Power of Questions on... (whatever issue is on the table)."

Once the person holding the question has been identified, they pose the question to the group, then they listen. The moderator sets a timer for five to ten minutes, and questions begin. When I was introduced to this activity, I was skeptical. How could a battery of questions do any good? But okay, it only takes a few minutes, so why not try it?

I was blown away.

The questions were *really* helpful. I wasn't the person bringing the dilemma, and yet I learned a lot. Hearing other people's questions showed me there were a plethora of perspectives and curiosities that I hadn't even considered. I learned just how narrow my focus was, even though I thought I was open-minded.

When the question time is up, the person presenting the dilemma reflects on the experience and, if they wish, shares what they learned or how they will move forward. Because the Power of Questions is simple and easy, you can use it in a variety of ways:

- at the start of a meeting to open up a generative space
- when you're stuck swirling around an issue
- near the end of a planning meeting or before you transition into the next phase of Adaptive Action

Our imaginary community center design team is stuck in the What? phase as we seek to identify our values. We've been swirling around the concept of mutual thriving. Juaquin proposes that we stop for a Power of Questions, and asks, "What does mutual thriving mean in the context of the programs we want to host in our community center?" I volunteer to moderate, set a timer and say, "Go!"

- *Why do we care about mutual thriving?*
- *In what ways does our community already support mutual thriving?*
- *What obstacles to mutual thriving might we encounter?*
- *How will we know if mutual thriving actually shows up in our work?*
- *In what ways would this project be affected if we don't prioritize mutual thriving?*
- *What are some ways we can engage people in thinking about mutual thriving?*
- *How is mutual thriving important for what we hope to accomplish?*
- *What is it about mutual thriving that makes it hard to discuss?*
- *Why are we swirling on this issue?*

When the Power of Questions ends, Juaquin thanks everyone for their questions and then engages in another approach to setting conditions for generativity. He tells a story about another project he was involved in and how a small group of people controlled the flow of information, cutting others out of important decisions. After telling his story, Juaquin expresses concerns about how power will be shared in the school we're designing. His story leads to an honest, vulnerable conversation about power and mutual thriving.

Storytelling is a potent, distinctly human pattern. We live our lives in story. Every day, every year, is a story. Every lifetime is too. Stories are humanity's way of organizing and sharing vital information. There is something about the beginning, middle, and end pattern, the plot, the crisis, the character development, that pulls us in. We can somehow understand that which we could not otherwise grasp.

Stories carry essential information such as dates, times, places, and people. But more importantly, they carry emotional and cultural information. Stories remind us of our common humanity. They help connect people. In Hawaiʻi, when people get together, even for business, they start by "talking story." We can set conditions for generativity by telling our own story and inviting others to tell theirs.

Storytelling is a great way to foster generativity. Old-school brainstorming is another, but hear me out. We've got to do it well, which isn't easy. Brainstorming can be highly generative, but it must be done within a truly protected space where even outlandish ideas are acceptable. Our team collectively commits to one simple rule: No feedback whatsoever.

No yeah-buts.

No "I like that."

None. At all.

Zip. Zero. Nada.

If a team can't do that, don't brainstorm. It does more harm than good. If a team does commit to doing it well, choose a few sentence stems, such as, "What if we..." or, "I'd like it if we..." or, "Maybe we could..." to get things rolling. Make sure someone takes good notes (or, as in the example below, do a silent brainstorm where everyone writes down their own ideas) and someone is a timekeeper. After the brainstorm is over, do not critique the ideas, as doing so can shut down future generativity. Instead, identify those you collectively want to explore.

In our imagined scenario, after Juaquin finishes his story, Nika suggests we brainstorm ways to ensure we establish and maintain equitable ways of sharing power. She offers to moderate a ten-minute silent brainstorm. Nika reviews the rules for brainstorming and asks if everyone present is willing to abide by them. All agree. Nika passes out pads of sticky notes and sets the timer. Everyone jots down their ideas, one per sticky note. When the timer rings, everyone takes their stickies and puts them up on a wall. Then everyone grabs a pen and puts a dot on the ideas they like best. We all stand back, looking for patterns in the dots. Five ideas are standouts.

"Do we all agree to move these five ideas forward in our planning process?" Nika asks. Heads nod. "Any objections?" No objections. Nika takes pictures of the five ideas and puts them in a digital folder named Maintaining Equitable Power.

For our fictional group, generativity has done its job. Now we need ways to agree it's time to close generativity and move to the next Adaptive Action phase. Often, doing so is just a matter of someone saying, "Seems like we can move on to So What?" or, "Are we ready to move into Now What? and make some decisions about action?" However, if there are unresolved issues or tensions, we need something more intentional. One way to close, as I mentioned earlier, is to use the Power of Questions. Offer to do so if anyone has any outstanding questions or dilemmas they'd like to explore before moving on.

Another way to close, especially if differing or opposing opinions are on the table, is to use a technique from Sociocracy, called governing by objection. Rather than voting or seeking consensus, in Sociocracy, people make decisions by revealing and addressing all objections. For those of us who revere majority rule, or who have come to embrace consensus as ideal, governance by objection sounds impossible. But even children successfully govern themselves with it. When faced with a stalemate, it's worth a try.

Here's a brief description. A decision is proposed, and whomever is facilitating the discussion asks for objections. Anyone who holds an objection states it, the reason for their objection, and how they would like their objection addressed. Let's imagine a subgroup designing the homeschooling program for our community center is meeting and the decision is proposed that parents will be expected to volunteer ten hours every week. A member of the subgroup states, "I object to this parental volunteer expectation. It's burdensome for many parents, and does not support our commitment to mutual thriving. I would be okay with either reducing the hours and spreading it out over a month, say thirty hours, or negotiating individually with each family."

Then members of the subgroup are polled for their response to the suggested solution. If they agree, they say, "I'm okay with that" or, "I can live with that." Or they could object, "I object to negotiating with each family as that will take a lot of time. Who will do it?"

Governing by objection may seem inefficient. So be it. Efficiency isn't the goal. Designing something genuinely adapted to local needs is.

You might find reason to use these approaches to moving from the first Adaptive Action phase to the second, or the second to the third, but you will likely find the Power of Questions or governing by objections comes in handy most in the Now What? phase. Deciding on actions, the third phase, can be tricky, especially if the group is large or inexperienced in these approaches. To bring closure in a tricky third phase, you can simply agree to go back to What? by asking "What are our options for action?"

Now that we've explored some ways to foster generativity in Adaptive Action and to bring closure, let's explore using Adaptive Action as a design process. The first step in Adaptive Action is to get a solid understanding of what you're designing. Is it educational programming for a rural community center? Are you designing a curriculum for primary age children to learn ecologically centered engineering principles? Maybe you're designing vocational learning opportunities for adolescents or an intergenerational regenerative school. Getting a clear description of What? is key to effective design. Here are some questions that work well in the What? phase:

- *What values will guide and shape our work?*
- *What is our vision for what we want to this school to be?*
- *In what ways will we support learners' interactions with an appreciation for nature?*
- *What Simple Rules do we commit to?*
- *What teaching and learning methods will we use to support self-becoming?*
- *What are our priorities?*
- *What containers do we need to operate in?*
- *What might we be unaware of?*
- *What groups of people do we want to be sure to include?*
- *What obstacles are we likely to face?*
- *What relevant patterns do we observe?*

The second phase of Adaptive Action is the So What? phase. In this the phase, you want to spend a good deal of time opening minds and hearts to what really matters. Don't rush So What? Allow time for everyone to noodle on questions like:

- *So what about how we'll run this school do we really care about?*
- *So what makes this project so important?*
- *So what questions could help us explore reciprocity more deeply?*
- *So what gets in the way of us collectively addressing volunteer expectations?*
- *So what resources are available to buy equipment?*
- *So what examples do we have of others addressing food security in a regenerative way?*

It is also important to incorporate design considerations in the So What? phase:

- *So what are the ways regenerative values could inform our process?*
- *So what might prevent everyone from thriving in the school we are designing?*
- *So what growth patterns should we be concerned about?*

- *So what are the important relationships we need to think about?*
- *So what networks are involved or need to be activated or engaged?*
- *So what is the big picture here?*
- *So what do we need to be sure we understand at the local or personal level?*
- *So what needs to be generated that does not already exist?*
- *So what are we hoping emerges from our process?*
- *So what conditions need to be set for that emergence to happen?*

Finally, we come to Now What? A quick reminder that in early Adaptive Action cycles, it is common to identify a few, easy to do, information-gathering action items, and then return to What? to start the next cycle. If you identify adding people to your decision-making process, you may very well need to repeat much of the discussions that were already had in the first Adaptative Action cycle. No worries. Revisiting discussions with new insights and perspectives is always useful.

Once ideas for action have been generated, rigorously examine them for alignment with Regenerative Values. Let's imagine that our community center planning group has identified the following as possible next actions:

- ask the city council for funding
- request a consultation with tribal leaders about potential collaboration
- begin holding workshops even though the building isn't finished
- start a virtual tool lending/sharing program while waiting to build a storage shed for community-owned tools
- set up a Go Fund Me or other online fundraising campaign

We set aside a half-day retreat to scrutinize each of these potential Now What? actions for alignment with reverence, reciprocity, and mutual thriving. Based on those discussions, we decide to approach tribal leaders, start the virtual tool lending program, and ask the city council for funding. We agree on actions for the next month and identify who will do them.

Keep the Design Cycle Going

At this point in the design process, things might seem very messy. That's okay. Return to What? and start the cycle again. The first few times I used Adaptive Action, I felt somewhat lost. I wanted at least an inkling of certainty about the outcome. I wanted checklists to be sure I covered all my bases. I wanted an end-of-process assessment that would tell me the outcome was a good one. But with Adaptive Action, there is no end to the process. Yes, in a few months our imaginary community center established a small workshop and tool lending library, but the efforts continued, and, in another year, we had a barebones community center with a fledgling afterschool program and operational homeschool cooperative.

However, there are always more decisions to make, more people to involve, more learning to set conditions for. So, we keep cycling through Adaptive Action. Some people on our planning team moved into other roles, such as facilitating the programs in the workshop or becoming a learner in the afterschool space. New people joined the planning team, bringing with them new wisdom, additional expertise, and fresh perspectives.

The most important thing to do when using Adaptive Action is to continue cycling through the phases until the structures and specifics of the design begin to take shape. If someone had advised me to do this ten years ago, I would have smiled politely, nodded, and ignored them, thinking, *That's just not how you design something!* But after seeing how time consuming, costly, and ineffective traditional strategic planning and common design practices are under conditions of high complexity, I now use Adaptive Action for all design processes, no matter what is being designed or how much has already been designed. Because Adaptive Action fosters generativity in the midst of dynamical change, *it* adapts as the school emerges and the design needs change. In that way, Adaptive Action mirrors the complex cycles of Earth. Ever changing and adapting, ongoing and generative.

It's a whole new (yet ancient) way of doing (and designing) school.

CHAPTER SUMMARY

Key Points

1. Regenerative schools are rooted in reverence, reciprocity, and mutual thriving, prioritize setting conditions conducive to life, and follow Rules for Regeneration.
2. Regenerative schools that emerge from the unique conditions in their locale will be resilient, relevant, and effective.
3. Design is tangible imagination. It is the intentional arrangement of elements, relationships, and patterns. *Collections* of *actions* and *elements* thoughtfully selected and arranged are powerful.
4. Design considerations are things we contemplate and play with, either in our minds or in our dialogue, or, most helpfully, in a sketch (I like to call them scribbles) that help us choose options that, working together, become more than the sum of their parts.
5. Rules for Regeneration, Regenerative Values, Complex Patterns, and CDE can serve as design considerations for regenerative schools.
6. Adaptive Action is an excellent method to use for regenerative design because it is intentionally generative and intended to help us work effectively in dynamic change.
7. Adaptive Action keeps going. Because Adaptive Action fosters generativity in the midst of dynamic change, *it* adapts as the school emerges and the design needs change and grow.

Playing with Complexity

At this point in your design process you may wish to revisit the What? and So What? phases to layer in the design considerations and ponder the questions from this chapter that might help you get a better description of what you're designing, the patterns involved, and the meaning of those patterns.

This is a good point to move on in earnest to the Now What? phase. If you're working alone, one of your Now What? steps might be to identify others you can share your ideas with. Perhaps it's just one person, a thought partner who can help you identify how to move your ideas out into the world. If you're already working as a group, what are your next steps to engaging a broader community? Or collaboration partners? Or people or organizations with needed resources?

Select a few ideas for fostering generativity and bringing generativity to closure and try them with others. Prioritize documentation and create a way for everyone to see the documentation. Think of it as more than taking notes or meeting minutes, think of it as creating a story that has a life of its own. Most importantly, keep going. Even small actions can have major influence.

PART III

SHIFTING TO A REGENERATIVE PARADIGM

10

How Systems Learn

So how do you change paradigms?...You keep pointing at the anomalies and failures in the old paradigm...with assurance from the new one, you insert people with the new paradigm in places of public visibility and power. You don't waste time with reactionaries; rather you work with active change agents and with the vast middle ground of people who are open-minded.

~ Donella Meadows, biologist, systems scientist

Force may make hypocrites, but it can make no converts.

~William Penn

One of my college professors told a story I've never forgotten. A revered elder was eating soup one day with one of his students. The teacher repeatedly tried reasoning with his student, but the young person argued every point. Finally, the old man stood up, leaned over the table and, with a wry smile, spit in the younger man's soup.

"Hey! Why did you do that? That's my lunch!"

The teacher sat down, still smiling. "I cannot change your mind. I cannot make you stop consuming the nonsense that makes you think the way you think. But I can spit in your soup, and that will make you think twice before you take another bite. Perhaps it will work with your thinking too."

This chapter is about soup spitting.

Or, more civilly, setting conditions for disruptive curiosity.

In Chapter 1, I wrote about how what Dr. Illah Nourbakhsh had said in Pittsburgh kept haunting my thoughts, that children should be producers of technology, not just consumers, and that he used technology to wage peace, not war.

That's soup spitting.

Dr. Nourbakhsh spat in my soup.

He didn't preach or taunt. He didn't lecture or argue. He adeptly tossed provocative ideas into my paradigmatic soup. He set conditions for disruptive curiosity.

If you're part of the growing number of people who are unhappy with education as we know it, it's easy to set your sights on either reforming what we've got or forcing collapse. Both options waste time and energy; the first because, as you know by now, reforms don't work, and the second because the conditions for collapse have been in place for decades and they're doing their job just fine, thank you very much.

I have no doubt that twenty years from now, schools will look nothing like education as we know it now, or as we've known it for the past two hundred years. Current education systems are so obsolete and rigid they cannot adapt to the complexities of our globally connected world.

They *will* collapse.

But I am not at all certain that what replaces education as we know it will emerge from a fundamentally different way of thinking, a *regenerative* way of thinking. There is every reason to believe that as different as future schools may look or operate, without a societal paradigm shift away from mechanistic, extractive, and exploitive ways of thinking, schools will continue to immerse generation after generation of young humans in the Rules of the Drill. The Rules of the Drill are just as easy to perpetuate online and with AI as they are in a schoolhouse. Probably easier.

Ending education as we know it isn't our concern.

Influencing a shift in the prevailing societal paradigm is.

Yes, we need people speaking up about how schools need

to change, but there is a far larger issue that needs attention: setting conditions for disrupting industrialism so the complex system we call society can learn to think in a whole new way, allowing a regenerative paradigm to emerge.

The Deets on Disruption

This book is about the relationship between education and the paradigm that shapes our society and how doing school in a whole new way can set conditions for a shift in the prevailing machine paradigm. Paradigm shifts are society's way of learning. They are fundamental changes. Changes that forever reorganize people's just-the-way-things-are assumptions. Such learning is not peripheral, it is central. Paradigm shifts are not tweaks or reform.

When Galileo advanced a sun-centric model of the solar system, it was such a radical reorganization of that society's beliefs that the Roman Catholic Church tried him for heresy, convicted him, and sentenced him to live out his life under house arrest. Galileo wasn't punished for proposing a reformed version of the Earth-centric model, but because he agreed with, and had generated evidence to support, the paradigm-shifting model proposed by Copernicus. Heliocentrism unseated the fundamental way ancient Roman society understood humanity's place in the universe.

Similarly, regenerative perspectives unseat the fundamental way industrial society understands humanity's place in the universe. A shift to regenerative thinking is no less disruptive to our society than was the shift to understanding the sun is the center of the solar system.

In my experience, people get very excited about paradigm-shifting disruption. Some folks think disruption is sexy, even fun.

It isn't.

The only things that need disrupting are tenaciously entrenched. Disrupting them is not only difficult, it's dangerous. Pushing for paradigm disruption without a solid understanding of how tricky it can be and without a potent replacement is ill-advised. Established systems, such as monetary, economic, health, political, and, yes, educational, push back hard when they're threatened. It's how complex systems protect themselves.

But wait. Paradigm shifts *require* disruption.

So, what to do?

Give up?

Maybe.

If the only method someone has to rattle existing paradigms is a bull-in-a-china-shop approach, it's best to walk away. That's how wars start. They only end when one side overwhelmingly overpowers the other. Not exactly an approach aligned with reverence, reciprocity, and mutual thriving. If you're this far in this book, however, you've got much better ways to influence complex change than violence. You know how to set conditions.

Even so, setting conditions for disruption is not for the faint of heart. I don't want to scare you, but I do want to be honest about how risky it can be. There is little applause for this level of changemaking. Galileo was convicted of heresy and sentenced to house arrest for nearly a decade because he affirmed a model of the solar system that is now taught to six-year-olds around the globe. If you're looking for a citizen of the year award, it's better to invest your efforts in polishing the status quo.

I don't say that sarcastically. Many people do good work that way.

What they don't do is set conditions for paradigmatic change.

And paradigmatic change is what humanity and Earth desperately need.

Disruptive Curiosity

Dabbling in disruption is like handling live grenades. It requires skill, patience, and finesse. Setting conditions for disruption is soup spitting. It intentionally interferes with established assumptions. It challenges perceived reality.

People don't like that.

Huh? experiences are disconcerting. Effective teachers know that setting conditions for disrupting individual learners' perceptions and assumptions requires compassion and patience. Disruption at the societal level requires even more compassion and patience.

That idea may surprise you.

It might even disrupt your idea of disruption. Bear with me.

I'm not saying we shy away from confronting the inhumanity of inhumane systems. To the contrary, setting conditions, by definition, means we act, and setting conditions for disruption usually means we act in ways that are contrary to what most people would consider "nice."

I doubt Galileo was nice.

But if we are committed to regenerative living, then Regenerative Values must guide our condition-setting actions, especially when we're setting conditions for disruption. Centering ourselves firmly in reverence, reciprocity, and a commitment to mutual thriving keeps us mindful of the potential harm disruption may cause and reminds us to find ways to dampen or mitigate that harm.

When we're considering how we might set conditions for society having a big, collective Huh? it's important to remember what we know about working with complex systems. Recall how in Chapter 8 we explored the difference between the parts of a complicated system (components) and those in a complex system (individuals). Also recall that the way we influence a complex system is by influencing the individuals that make up the whole. There are examples of how this works everywhere. Let's consider one from one of my favorite places on the California Coast.

If you ever get a chance to visit the Monterey Bay Aquarium, do it. One of their large tanks is home to a sizeable school of Pacific sardines. Watching them move as one is mesmerizing. If you do visit, look up the feeding schedule, and don't miss it. When krill are dropped into the tank, the fish nearest the food move quickly toward it. Then the entire school shifts, changing shape as the fish move to gobble up the food. If larger fish approach the school, sardines on the edges change directions, and the entire school morphs, again changing its shape, speed, and path.

Like I said, it's mesmerizing. It's like watching a murmuration of starlings underwater.

The whole complex system changes when a few individuals change direction. It doesn't take a lot to change the entire system, just a handful of krill, or some grouper nosing a few sardines. *The shifts never happen by force*. I often hear people talk about disruption in terms of brute force. But as William Penn said, "Force may make hypocrites, but it can make no converts."

We don't need more hypocrites.

We need converts.

Lots of converts.

Converts from every age, race, occupation, nationality, religion, culture, political ideology, education level, and economic status.

Upending family gatherings by trying to get your relatives to see your point of view does not set conditions for effective disruption. As Dr. Meadows says in the quote at the start of this chapter, don't waste your time with reactionaries.

Don't be one either.

The key to setting conditions for paradigmatic change is to help lots of people have Huh? experiences that leave them curious and questioning assumptions. That kind of curiosity requires vulnerability, and vulnerability can't happen unless people feel, at least to some degree, safe.

Creating conditions for disruptive curiosity is tricky. A part of our brains, the amygdala, spends all its time, day and night, scanning the environment for anything potentially threatening. Fundamentally, it asks, "Am I going to die?" It answers that question by scouting about for anything different. Any out-of-the-ordinary difference triggers further scrutiny, which heightens anxiety. Marian, the fourth grader in Chapter 7, and Beth, her teacher, were both triggered by something out of the ordinary. For Marian, the out-of-the-ordinary difference was her father going on a longer business trip than he had gone on before, and for Beth it was an upset Marian.

Here's the pickle.

Setting conditions for disruption requires an out-of-the ordinary difference that triggers the amygdala, setting off fight, flight, freeze, or fawn responses, when, instead, we want people to feel curious. The job of the paradigm changemaker is to figure out how to set conditions for out-of-the-ordinary differences while creating and maintaining safety. When Aisha's family took her to the zoo, they changed the container from her familiar home to an out-of-the-ordinary container, filled with out-of-the-ordinary creatures. One way to think about Aisha's insistence that the elephant was a dog is to see it as her way of maintaining the safety of the ordinary. When her uncle pointed out all the differences between the out-of-the-ordinary four-legged beast and an ordinary doggy, Aisha's amygdala was triggered. There was no way to emphasize out-of-the-ordinary differences without making her amygdala light up.

Aisha's uncle dampened her potential fear response with his own warm presence. He acted out of reverence for his little niece. He didn't shout at her, nor did he insult her or tell her she was wrong. He compassionately pointed out the differences and used his own presence and proximity to create a safe container for her to wrestle with the unexpected differences she had encountered. When she did not accept her uncle's perspective, he didn't insist. He didn't use his outsized power to force her to agree.

Whomever we want to influence, we need to use the same approach. We don't want hypocrites. We need converts. We influence the whole by influencing individuals, and we don't create coverts with force.

I learned this lesson near the end of my term on the board of the National Association for the Education of Young Children. When I was elected vice president, I had no idea I would be responsible for board oversight of a massive restructuring of the organization's relationship with its (then) nearly three hundred affiliate nonprofits. The restructuring process took almost the entirety of my four-year term.

During the process, we dramatically changed the requirements for affiliation, including a new mandate that each would-be affiliate had to report, in detail, how it adhered to and advanced the national organization's diversity, inclusivity, and equity initiative. Called HPIO, the initiative had been born of good intentions years before but was mostly a statement few people read or followed. By the time I joined the national board, I had heard the term HPIO often, but, even though I served as an officer of the Arizona state affiliate, I had no idea that HPIO stood for High Performing Inclusive Organization, much less what it meant to our work at the national, state, or local level. We were inadvertently following the simple rule: HPIO is something we say but do not do.

Those of us on the reaffiliation committee were committed to making sure HPIO was something we not only said but did. We wanted our affiliated organizations to embrace early educators of every cultural, racial, gender, and demographic background in specific and meaningful ways. To affiliate, we required compliance.

We forced the issue.

After the restructuring was done, affiliate leaders met for Affiliate Day at the national organization's annual conference. The staff member overseeing affiliates at the national office asked leaders from three organizations who had gone through the reaffiliation process to present a breakout session on how the process played out in their organizations and how they had met the new criteria.

I was eager to hear how affiliates had prioritized HPIO, but during the breakout session, none of the speakers mentioned it. When the presenters asked for questions, I raised my hand and asked if each leader could describe how their organization was implementing HPIO. The speakers looked at each other, presumably, I thought, to decide who would go first. Instead, each shrugged and no one answered.

Finally, the leader facilitating the session said, "We've been so busy becoming a high performing organization, we decided we needed to take care of that first *before* we tackled inclusivity."

I was gobsmacked.

Exasperated.

Flat-out speechless.

After all those long hours we had spent figuring out how we would require our affiliates to make a major shift in their responsibilities toward non-white, non-female, non-straight, and younger early educators, they still didn't get it. I was tempted to deliver a full-throated rebuke. It certainly would have been justified.

But how would that set conditions for disruptive curiosity?

How would a coercive response, however valid, create a safe container for people to question their priorities, their habits, their confidence that they were indeed champions of equity and inclusivity? I sat silently through the remainder of the Q & A, wanting to respond but not knowing what to say. One thought, and variations on its theme, bounced around in my mind:

> We get to the HP through the I.
> The path to high performance is through inclusivity.
> We can't be high performing if we're not inclusive.
> *We get to the HP through the I.*

I decided to spit in our collective soup. I raised my hand. "I want to comment on the idea that affiliates need to become high performing *before* becoming inclusive," I said. "That's backwards.

We've got to shift our thinking. Inclusivity isn't an add-on. It isn't something we do only after we have our act together. We get to the HP through the I. We are only high performing if we're first inclusive."

The session ended, and we returned to the main conference room. I didn't want to be there. I was deeply shaken. I felt like Sisyphus, futilely pushing that proverbial boulder uphill. The large group meeting started with a report out from breakout sessions. Someone who had been in our session raised their hand and said, "I want to talk about what Ida Rose said in our breakout. She said that the way to the HP in HPIO is through the I. I don't know that we all get that. I know I don't know how to make that a reality, but I think it is important. We need to talk about that."

Thus began a genuine conversation about what it means to fully include everyone, and how that leads to affiliates being the kind of organizations we all wanted them to be. We might not have thought of that conversation in terms of Regenerative Values, but at its core, we were discussing how we wanted reverence, reciprocity, and mutual thriving to show up for all early educators in our affiliates. I had spent hours over several years working with our committee, national staff, and leaders across the country to figure out how to require affiliates to embrace and authentically enact HPIO. That requirement perpetuated lip service. But a few well-placed sentences made it difficult to keep eating the status quo soup.

Forcing affiliate leaders to embrace HPIO created hypocrites.
Setting conditions for disruptive curiosity invited converts.

Setting Conditions for Disruptive Curiosity

Much of what we've explored in earlier chapters can be used to expertly set conditions for disruptive curiosity. For example, we can use the CDE framework. Recall how Aisha experienced different exchanges when her family changed the container. The exchanges Aisha had with her uncle likely could not have happened in the familiar containers of her home or his.

Think about the practice field you created in Part 2 in terms of how you can influence containers, differences, and exchanges that could lead to disruptive curiosity. What might happen if you changed containers? Or if you rearranged a meeting to facilitate exchanges between people that wouldn't normally interact? Something as simple as changing seating arrangements can make a meaningful difference. If you keep all your "experts" on the stage or seated at VIP tables, you limit meaningful exchanges with the majority of individuals that make up the complex systems you're trying to influence.

How might you use CDE to influence your own perspectives? Remember the young Latina way back in Chapter 2 who stood and asked Sylvia Acevedo if Girl Scouts was real? She actively sought disconfirming information. To provoke our own disruptive curiosity, we need to do the same. For several years now, I've made it a practice at any gathering to sit and talk with people I don't know. I do this because I know that interacting primarily with people I know, and especially people who share my beliefs and worldview, reifies my own thinking and isolates me from differences and exchanges that can prompt me to think in whole new ways.

I want to keep thinking in whole new ways.

I want to set conditions for disruptive curiosity in my own life.

Whether you're setting conditions for disruptive curiosity for yourself or for others, one of the most powerful things you can do is ask questions. The kinds of questions that set conditions for disruptive curiosity are the kind we explored in Chapter 9. Powerful questions are open-ended and invite curiosity. I often pose inquiry as, "I'm wondering...."

Experiences can also lead people to Huh? moments. We now live in rural Arizona where residential solar power and electric vehicles are beginning to catch on, but many folks see the shift as a threat to their way of life. Our youngest son, David, is a construction superintendent for a large commercial contractor. He drives a gas-powered company truck equipped with an electric motor that engages at starts and stops to save fuel. There's a switch on the dashboard that activates that feature. David told me that several colleagues have climbed into his truck, noticed he had the electric motor engaged, and before they're even seated, they hit the switch to turn it off. David smiles, turns it back on, and says, "My truck. My rules."

I don't get it, but many people feel this way, including the retired contractor we hired to build some fences and insulate a shed for us. We are one of the first people in Arizona to own an electric tractor. We charge it overnight with our residential solar system and get six to eight hours of run time. James, the contractor, teased me about our wimpy tractor, saying there was no way it could do the work of a similarly sized diesel John Deere.

I just shrugged. Absent disruptive curiosity, why argue?

One day, while James and his son were working at our place, I started removing a few stumps and digging a swale with the tractor's backhoe. After a while, James walked over.

"How long have you been out here on that thing?"

"About an hour."

"It's so quiet, I didn't even hear it." James looked at the loose stumps lying on the dirt. "Did you do all this? Right now? With this thing?"

"Yes sir, I did."

James eyed the tractor front to rear. "Hmm. Is it running? There's no exhaust."

"James, it's electric."

"Well, I know that. I just hadn't given it any thought that there would be no exhaust. That's pretty nice. I hate tractor exhaust. I'm surprised it did all this work. That's pretty hard clay you dug through. So how do you power the thing? You're off-grid here."

"Sunshine, James. Sunshine."

"But what's its run time? Can't be very long."

"We charge it off our batteries overnight, and it runs all day. Runs like a Deere, James."

"Well, I'll be."

Experiences have a way of spitting in status quo soup for you.

No need to argue or reason with. No need to prove your point. The experience proves it for you. I've written a lot about how changing containers can expose people to different exchanges and experiences. But in this example, it was important that the container *wasn't* different. It would be one thing for James to see an electric tractor at a trade show in San Francisco. It was quite another for him to see it operating, off-grid, doing real work right in his own community.

When considering how you might set up experiences that can spark disruptive curiosity, think carefully about how people might engage in those experiences within familiar containers. When starting a school, you may need approval by some kind of governing board. Or you might be in the process of setting conditions for parents and interested community members to self-organize around the idea of regenerative education. Can you arrange a learning journey in your own community where policymakers or parents can experience schools similar to what you're designing?

Learning journeys can be incredibly powerful because they create stories. Remember, for humans, story is the most powerful of complex patterns. If you want to set conditions for disruptive curiosity, create stories. Stories help us think in a whole new way. They make new ideas come alive in real scripts and scenes, helping our imaginations move from abstraction to reality. Stories allow us to play with new ideas in ways that invite disruptive curiosity without invoking fear. They allow us to try on the machine paradigm bedeviling notion that humans are fundamentally responsible for making intelligent contributions to the continuation of life on Earth, all from the safety of the familiar.

With the Full Assurance of the New Paradigm

If you've read this book from the beginning, you're probably aware by now that by merely designing a regenerative school, much less opening one, you're going to encounter pushback.

Lots of pushback. Dr. Peter Gray, psychologist and play advocate, studies nontraditional schools. In his book *Evidence that Self-Directed Education Works*, Dr. Gray says that parents find negative feedback from others as the primary downside of "unschooling."

Designing and implementing a regenerative school is one of the most paradigm-disruptive things we can do because it challenges both the prevailing societal paradigm and the schools that perpetuate it. Remember, though the prevailing machine paradigm and our educational institutions promote complication, they are complex systems. They reciprocally reinforce each other. Industrialism gives schools a purpose (produce a workforce), and schools give the machine paradigm its most valuable asset: a workforce educated just enough to make industrial capitalism work. Redefining schools as places set aside for any kind of learning is inherently disruptive to both the paradigm and schools.

But disruption is never all it takes for paradigms to shift. Repeatedly pointing out the inadequacies of the existing paradigm is necessary, but it is also insufficient. In Chapter 2, I cited Dr. Thomas Kuhn, the science philosopher who coined the term *paradigm*. In his study of scientific revolutions, Dr. Kuhn found that attempts to disrupt a paradigm without a well-articulated superior replacement failed. The new paradigm must do a better job explaining the phenomena under question than the existing one does.

Over the last twenty years, as I've explored complexity thinking and sustainable ways of living, I've come to know many people who long for a new regenerative paradigm to emerge. People want ways of thinking and living that revere all of nature, including each other. We long for equitable economic systems, grounded in an unwavering commitment to mutual thriving. Still, very few people want to admit that education as we know it perpetuates the existing exploitative paradigm. Even fewer see schools as the place to start if we want generations of humans to be grounded in the complex ways the world works, and who value reverence, reciprocity, and mutual thriving.

But if we truly want to set conditions for a new paradigm to emerge, we need to start with schools. Regenerative schools, popping up here and there, create the critical momentum that we need to free society from the machine paradigm's tenacious grip. When schools everywhere demonstrate that non-traditional, intergenerational places of learning grounded in reverence, reciprocity, and mutual thriving do a better job of educating humans young and old and create peace, prosperity, and a regenerated, flourishing planet, a new paradigm will become impossible to ignore.

For that kind of momentum to become reality, if we want the complex systems that make up our complex society to learn a whole new way of thinking, we need large numbers of people committed to disrupting the machine paradigm's grip on their own thinking and to establishing a whole new regenerative way of doing school.

11

E HOʻI MAI ʻOE (COME BACK)

The view of reality emerging now is breathtakingly new to those of us who have been shaped by the Industrial Growth Society. Supported by postmodern science and ancient spiritual traditions, it brings a fresh understanding of our relationship to the world and of powers within us for its healing. Liberating us from constricted notions of who we are and what we need, it brings us home to our true nature— in league with the stars and trees of our thrumming universe.

~ JOANNA MACY & MOLLY BROWN

The winter of 2023 dumped over ten feet of snow on Northern Arizona, more snow than any winter in the previous seventy-five years. From January through March, my husband Rick and I looked longingly out the windows of our temporary travel-trailer home, eagerly awaiting spring so we could build our off-grid homestead in earnest.

Finally, in early April, warmish weather tiptoed onto the Kaibab Plateau south of the Grand Canyon where we live. We donned warm work clothes and headed out to build garden beds, and create swales and check dams to capture precious precipitation. On that crisp Saturday morning, as I positioned our electric tractor's backhoe to remove a stump where a garden bed would go, a mockingbird chirped his repertoire, filling the air with the promise of spring.

Like dozens of times before, I positioned our electric tractor so I could dig out a stump and went through the backhoe setup sequence: turn off the tractor, set the parking brake, put three levers in neutral, get off, stand next to the tractor, and start the tractor again. I knew the sequence better than the flag poem.

This time, however, when I pulled down the hand throttle to power up the backhoe hydraulics, the two-ton machine lurched out of stationary mode and jumped the parking brake. Driving forward at full throttle, something that should have been impossible without a person in its seat, the tractor knocked me to the ground. The large rear tire ran over my right leg, crushing it from ankle to groin, snapping and splintering my femur. Driverless, the tractor hurtled toward the county road south of our home, stopped only by a hulking juniper in its path.

I looked up. Everything around me seemed draped in a surreal haze. I became inexplicably calm. Grateful for shock-induced endorphins I breathed deeply and began talking to myself.

Focus on your breath.

In. Out. Deep. Slow.

Stay present. Stay awake.

In. Out. Deep. Slow.

I glanced at my thigh. It was strangely flat.

I felt my pants for blood. They were dry.

I remembered what I had learned about the dangers of internal bleeding from femur breaks and knew I needed immediate emergency medical help. Rick called 911, but the call failed. I lifted my head and suggested he back up to get aligned with the cell phone tower and try again. This time the call went through.

We live thirty-five miles from the nearest hospital. Fortunately, ten minutes down the highway, locals had long ago established a well-staffed volunteer fire department. Within minutes, multiple emergency vehicles descended on our property and over a dozen High Country Fire Rescue volunteers ran to my side.

As luck would have it, it was a training day.

The emergency personnel worked quickly, evaluating my injuries and working hard to start IVs. In my early thirties,

I had survived ovarian cancer. Chemo had wrecked my veins, so even phlebotomists working in an ideal environment can have trouble starting an IV.

"Hard jab!" called out a young paramedic. "Yes! It's in. No! Damn! It failed." He pulled out the needle, throwing it to the ground, and grabbed another.

I raised my head. "It's okay," I said. "Do whatever you have to do. My veins are hard to find, and they wiggle."

"It's going to hurt," he told me.

"I know. It's okay. Do what you gotta do. I'm fine." I resumed my internal dialogue.

Breathe. In. Out. Deep. Slow. Stay present. Stay awake.

As they worked, everyone's face was taut, brows furrowed, lips tight. After a couple more tries, IVs were secured in the back of both my hands. A man with an iPad approached Captain Robert Trotter who had been with me from the moment he arrived.

"Are we gonna drive or fly?" he asked.

"Fly!" The urgency in Captain Trotter's voice surprised me.

Well, okay then. My concerns were valid. I could be bleeding internally.

Other members of the emergency crew brought over a backboard and gurney.

"This is gonna hurt," Captain Trotter said, "but we'll move you as fast as we can. Take a deep breath."

They put the gurney on the ground next to me, slid the board under my back, put on a neck brace, and lifted me. Meanwhile someone maneuvered an ambulance closer, driving through mucky melting patches of snow. The EMS team lifted the gurney, expecting the wheel mechanism to unfold under it so they could roll me to the ambulance, but one side stuck. They had to jiggle the gurney (and me) to get the wheels to drop.

Silly me. I thought childbirth hurt.

With the wheels down, we went bumpity-bump over rocky, muddy ground. They lifted me into the ambulance while someone said the chopper was enroute and would land just off the highway, a half mile from our home. The paramedic quickly got pain meds flowing. I looked at the faces of everyone in the ambulance. Their set jaws and furrowed brows reflected the serious reality, but I desperately needed some smiles.

Just then Captain Trotter leaned in and said, "Ma'am, I need to cut off your bra. May I?"

Darn.

My favorite overalls and comfy winter work boots had already succumbed to emergency shears. But this was a brand-new bra. A pretty bra at that. When it comes to undergarments, I'm a no-nonsense kind of gal, but over the long winter, I had found an adorable lavender bra printed with seahorses and coral reefs and decided, why not? That day was the first time I had worn it.

"Of course," I replied, "but before you do, may I ask you something?"

"Sure," he said.

"Is it cute?"

"What?"

"My bra. Is it cute?"

He chuckled. "Yes, it's cute."

The paramedic who'd had such trouble starting my IVs moved closer. "Wait! I wanna see it!" He said. "Okay! That's definitely one cute bra!"

Everyone laughed. Including me.

When Systems Run Amok

Since the accident, I've struggled to find words for how I feel. I will never forget how the ground held me where I fell, nestled in juniper needles. My gratitude for the emergency volunteers who cared for me so kindly and professionally runs deep. I feel enormously fortunate to be alive. But there is another emotion I feel just as strongly as these. For months, I couldn't name it. But when I had recovered enough to finish writing this book, the feeling revealed itself.

Betrayal.

I remember lying on the ground, shocked that a cutting-edge machine, intended to be kind to Earth, a machine I had painstakingly searched for, waited for, and learned to use, had malfunctioned and hurt me so horrifically. I feel betrayed that a manufacturer that brands itself as committed to caring for Earth, to using science and engineering to create sustainable ways of growing food, had sold me a machine that malfunctioned and caused me such grave harm. I recognized that feeling as I started writing again because it is familiar.

It's what I feel about education as we know it.

Betrayed.

When I became a professional educator, I never imagined the pain and inhumanity I would witness in hundreds of classrooms, in dozens of policy and admin meetings, and in my own children's lives. The machine paradigm, and the schools that perpetuate it, was supposed to make our world a better place. Industrial capitalism promises to create prosperous societies with centralized electricity, water, and sanitation supplied to modest but adequate homes, with access to healthcare and free education so children can also grow up to be productive citizens.

But the machine paradigm has betrayed us. Between wars and oil catastrophes, hatred for some cultures and races and privilege for others, rampant homelessness and inequitable access to resources based on wealth and perceived worthiness, there is abundant evidence that the machine paradigm has run roughshod over our planet, crushing our humanity, and causing incalculable harm. Schools, as we know them, in service of the paradigm, do the same day in and day out, year after year.

I don't merely write from a bleeding heart. For decades, I've witnessed the harm schools cause firsthand. I'm thinking of Ryan, an eleven-year-old autistic boy with profound intellectual disabilities who was booted out of the program he had attended since preschool when the district I worked for closed the center where his class was housed. Special education administrators had dumped him into a neighborhood school without conducting the legally mandated evaluation of his needs. They did this, not because anyone who knew Ryan thought it was a good idea, but because it was part of a broader scheme for the district to make money off of special education.

I'm thinking about the small, second grade Black boy whom I saw repeatedly struck by a much larger Caucasian child in the presence of their teacher, who not only didn't protect the smaller child, but blamed him for disrupting her class when he told the bully to back off. I'm thinking of the friends, colleagues, and acquaintances who have shared their stories of humiliation or abuse at school, or their frustration as parents at not being able to get their children's schools to respond humanely to commonsense requests.

I'm thinking of the meeting I had with my oldest son's seventh-grade science teacher. After several years of homeschooling, I found myself a single mom of three preadolescent kids, working again as a public school psychologist, and George found himself in an overcrowded Southern California middle school with a science teacher who always seemed annoyed with him. Mr. Abe emailed me and asked that I bring George to meet with him after school. George's behavior, his email said, was unacceptable.

Our meeting was brief and to the point. Mr. Abe was upset because George questioned just about everything he said.

Oh dear. In our homeschool, I used the Socratic method, a pedagogical approach to critical thinking that encourages learners to question the adequacies of ideas. His teacher did not see George's questions as critical thinking. He saw them as rude and disruptive. Mr. Abe reminded me he taught over a hundred and twenty students daily, and he had a curriculum to cover. He had no time or patience for George's interruptions.

George and I walked to my car while I contemplated how to tell him that teachers might not appreciate the way I had taught him to question everything. As we stepped off the curb into the parking lot, George stopped, dropped his backpack, and stared at the ground.

"Oh hon. It will be okay," I said. "Let's go home and talk."

"Mom," he turned to me, tears welling up. "You know what's wrong with this place?" I wanted to tell him that indeed I did but chose instead to listen.

"They don't give you time to think. You're rushed from one class to the next. Fifty minutes of history, then seven minutes to run to your locker and get to algebra. No time to think about what you just learned in history. No time to think about what you're going to learn in math. Mom, I just need time to think."

His words crushed my heart then like my tractor would later crush my leg.

I know I'm not the only person with eyes on this page who has been crushed by education as we know it and by the industrial worldview it supports. Beyond what I have witnessed and the stories I've been told, there are countless examples of the damage done to people and planet.

The pain is real.

The harm runs deep.

Healing Can Be Ours

I have a plan for healing my trauma, and I invite you to consider it for healing yours. Compost. That's right. Complicated, extractive ways teach us to fight back, to retaliate, or remain strong and overcome. But if we overcome by the same means and values that caused harm in the first place, we cause more damage.

We can let betrayal keep us angry and stuck, or we can toss it in our heart's compost heap and let it decompose into useful grief. Grieving doesn't just immerse us in pain. It reminds us of what we love and have lost. Grief calls us to return to a way of being and living we might only know from long-forgotten dreamlike memories.

E ho'i mai 'oe. Come back.

Industrialism has so robbed us of the wonder of our own humanity, it seems impossible to find our way home. But that is exactly what we must do. We must regenerate our own humanity, allowing grief to call us back to ways of thinking, living, and being that may be wholly new to us but are as ancient as the land and sea.

E ho'i mai 'oe. Come back.

Return to our love of Earth and all Earth holds.

Return to our responsibility to make intelligent contributions for sustaining life on Earth.

Return to reverence, reciprocity, and a steadfast commitment to mutual thriving.

Those of us who want a flourishing planet must commit to a whole new way of thinking, learning, living, and raising future generations. That sounds like a tall order. But just like a large school of sardines can take off in an entirely new direction when a handful of fish shift their trajectories, individual humans can shift their course and affect society, even all of humanity. Human systems learn and change from small efforts, here, there, and everywhere. In off-the-beaten-path places, in backyards and libraries, in community centers and living rooms.

Healing the harm caused by industrial schooling can happen anywhere.

Wild Heart Farm, located about two hours north of Phoenix, is nestled against an embankment of a riparian ecosystem, dotted with towering cottonwoods. Nearly a year after my tractor ran me over, on a windy afternoon, I visited the farm as part of a permaculture design certification course I was taking at Northern Arizona University. Our class spent a few hours learning about regenerating soil using cover crops, and how to create food forests. There was a composting toilet on site, and we saw firsthand what six-month aged humanure (manure made from human feces) looks and smells like (it looked like gorgeous soil and had no noxious smell). We learned about no-till growing methods and how to make fertilizer tea from comfrey.

As the day drew to a close, everyone sat on the ground in a closing circle. I wanted to join, but I knew my leg was still too weak to get down and up again with any degree of dignity. In the few seconds it took me to decide, nope, not sitting on the ground, three people jumped up to help me. One grabbed a chair and brought it over as everyone scooched around to make a place for me to sit.

As the wind wafted through the cottonwoods and the waning sun warmed my face, I felt profoundly connected. In our circle, several of us were elders. Some of us were a decade or so younger. About half the group were university students, most in their early twenties. One was there with his mother, who lived nearby. One in our group, who was also there with her mother, one of our professors, was six years old. Here we were, young and old, of different genders, a mosaic of racial backgrounds and nationalities, all learning together how to resuscitate Earth and grow food on a precious patch of land.

I smiled. *This* was a regenerative school, practicing reverence, reciprocity, and mutual thriving. We were all learners and teachers. Everyone participating, asking questions, spreading compost, delighting in the fairy door discovered by our six-year-old classmate. There was no externally mandated curriculum. No separating by age or knowledge or skill or supposed ability. No "discipline" problems or grades or tests.

Just joy.

I closed my eyes and allowed betrayal to decompose in the warm compost of the regenerative learning community we had collectively cultivated. My heart pulsed with the same tender longing I had felt years before on Maui. As I said at the beginning of this book, the kind of educational change we long for will take a considerable number of us developing a nuanced understanding of *why* schools have such great influence on society, and *how* educational systems change.

I hope you are in that number.

I hope that when the deep longing for *what* our schools could be rises within you, that you feel tender and hopeful, like I did at

Pūnana Leo O Maui and at Wild Heart Farm. I also hope you find a community who lives regenerative values, where you can compost the pain caused when industrialized society runs roughshod over people. I hope that you take your profound longing and wrap it around you as a sacred cloth, holding you safe and close through what will likely be a bumpy ride to a profoundly important destination: a whole new way of doing school.

INDEX

D

E

About the Author

Ida Rose Florez, Ph.D., is a learning scientist, systems-change expert, and educational psychologist whose focus is revitalizing regenerative practices in schools. She writes for popular, trade, and academic publications and engages audiences through workshops and keynote speeches across the US and internationally. She lives in Williams, Arizona.

ABOUT NEW SOCIETY PUBLISHERS

New Society Publishers is an activist, solutions-oriented publisher focused on publishing books to build a more just and sustainable future. Our books offer tips, tools, and insights from leading experts in a wide range of areas.

We're proud to hold to the highest environmental and social standards of any publisher in North America. When you buy New Society books, you are part of the solution!

At New Society Publishers, we care deeply about *what* we publish—but also about *how* we do business.

- This book is printed on 100% **post-consumer recycled paper**, processed chlorine-free, with low-VOC vegetable-based inks (since 2002)
- Our corporate structure is an innovative employee shareholder agreement, so we're one-third employee-owned (since 2015)
- We've created a Statement of Ethics (2021). The intent of this Statement is to act as a framework to guide our actions and facilitate feedback for continuous improvement of our work
- We're carbon-neutral (since 2006)
- We're certified as a B Corporation (since 2016)
- We're Signatories to the UN's Sustainable Development Goals (SDG) Publishers Compact (2020–2030, the Decade of Action)

To download our full catalog, sign up for our quarterly newsletter, and to learn more about New Society Publishers, please visit newsociety.com.

ENVIRONMENTAL BENEFITS STATEMENT

New Society Publishers saved the following resources by printing the pages of this book on chlorine free paper made with 100% post-consumer waste.

TREES	WATER	ENERGY	SOLID WASTE	GREENHOUSE GASES
30 FULLY GROWN	2,400 GALLONS	13 MILLION BTUs	100 POUNDS	12,900 POUNDS

Environmental impact estimates were made using the Environmental Paper Network Paper Calculator 4.0. For more information visit www.papercalculator.org